210M   Pro Tools Music Production Techniques

Copyright and Disclaimer

Trademarks

Acknowledgments

Avid Worldwide Training would like to thank all Avid Certified Instructors for their ongoing suggestions and comments, based on their experience in the classroom and their professional editing expertise, which have resulted in the continued improvement of Avid courseware. The footage/music provided with this book is to be used only to complete the exercises contained herein. Rights are not granted to use the footage in any commercial or non-commercial production or video.

Exercise Session:

"Rococo"

Written and Performed by Arcade Fire

PT210M, Version 10

PN: 9329-65185-00

ISBN-13: 000-0-000000-00-0

Table of Contents

Preface

Pro Tools 210M: Music Production Techniques is a three-day course that covers specific techniques for working with Avid® Pro Tools® 10 in a professional music production environment. The main topics in this course are followed by exercises that allow you to practice concepts taught in class.

Upon successful completion of 200-series coursework, you will be eligible to take the Avid *Pro Tools Operator Certification* exam. For more information on Pro Tools certification, visit the Avid Training and Education website at http://www.avid.com/support/training.

Prerequisites for This Course

This course requires successful completion of the first 200-series course, entitled *Pro Tools 201: Pro Tools Production II*. Each 200-series course assumes a basic understanding of computers and their operation, digital audio and MIDI recording concepts, and Pro Tools software fundamentals.

Pro Tools Training Path

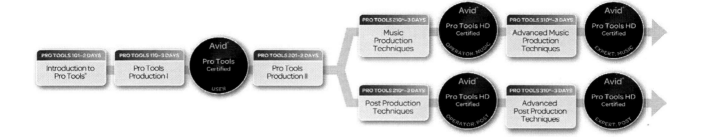

Worksurface Training Path

VENUE Training Path

Conventions and Symbols Used in This Guide

Procedures and Lists

Procedures and lists appear in one of the following forms:

1 Numbered procedures and lists are used when the order of steps or items is critical.

   – Bulleted procedures and lists are used when the order of steps or items is not critical, or when only one step or item is required.

Menu and Key Commands

The following are examples of the conventions used in this guide to indicate menu choices and keyboard commands:

Convention	Action
File > Save Session	Choose Save Session from the File menu
Control+N	Hold down the Control key and press the N key
Command-click	Hold down the Command key and click the mouse button
Right-click (Windows)	Click with the right mouse button
Press [1]	Press 1 on the Numeric keypad

Icons

The following icons are used to call attention to tips, important notices, shortcuts, cross-references, and examples.

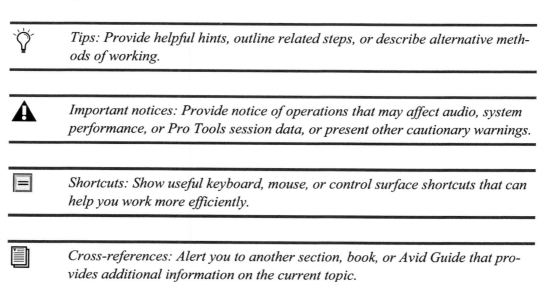

Tips: Provide helpful hints, outline related steps, or describe alternative methods of working.

Important notices: Provide notice of operations that may affect audio, system performance, or Pro Tools session data, or present other cautionary warnings.

Shortcuts: Show useful keyboard, mouse, or control surface shortcuts that can help you work more efficiently.

Cross-references: Alert you to another section, book, or Avid Guide that provides additional information on the current topic.

Cross-Platform Issues

This course book applies to both Mac OS and Windows Pro Tools systems. Most Pro Tools controls and tools look the same on both systems, most procedures are identical, and most menu items are the same. There are, however, some differences in keyboard commands and file naming conventions that are helpful to know if you use different platforms or move sessions between platforms.

Keyboard Commands

Many keyboard commands in Pro Tools use *modifier keys*, which are keys pressed in combination with other keys or with a mouse action. In addition, other equivalent keys have different names on each platform. The following table summarizes equivalent keys on Mac OS and Windows:

Mac OS	Windows
COMMAND KEY	CTRL (CONTROL) KEY
OPTION KEY	ALT KEY
CTRL (CONTROL) KEY	START (WIN) KEY
RETURN KEY	ENTER KEY ON MAIN (NOT NUMERIC) KEYPAD
DELETE KEY	BACKSPACE KEY

File Naming Conventions

There are some differences in the way files are named and recognized by Mac OS and Windows.

File Name Extensions

For cross-platform compatibility, all files in a session must have a 3-letter file extension added to the file name. Session files for Pro Tools software versions 7.x and later have the extension ".ptf", 5.1-6.9 session files have the extension ".pts," and Pro Tools 5 sessions have the extension ".pt5." WAV files have the ".wav" file extension, and AIFF files have the ".aif" file extension.

Incompatible ASCII Characters

Pro Tools file names cannot use ASCII characters that are incompatible with either system. The following characters should not be used in order to maintain cross-platform compatibility:

/ (*forward slash*)　\ (*backslash*)　: (*colon*)　* (*asterisk*)　? (*question mark*)　" (*quotation marks*)

' (*apostrophe*)　< (*less-than symbol*)　> (*greater-than symbol*)　| (*vertical line or pipe*)

Any character typed with the Command key on the Mac OS.

System Compatibility Information

Students should have access to a Pro Tools HD 10.0 (or later) system to complete the exercises. The exercises also require the use of a MIDI keyboard controller and various virtual instrument plug-ins. The exercises should be completed on a control surface if possible.

Pro Tools System Configurations

This course book provides some basic information about Pro Tools system configurations. For specific requirements and details on working with your Pro Tools system, consult your course instructor.

The installation and connection of Pro Tools software and hardware are beyond the scope of this course, and should be done by a qualified technician or course instructor. Complete installation and configuration instructions are included with each Avid product.

210-Level Exercises

In this course (as well as the 310M course) step-by-step workflows are provided where new concepts are introduced in exercises. However, students are expected to have attained a certain level of proficiency in Pro Tools before taking these courses (in particular the techniques covered in the 101, 110, and 201 courses). As such, tasks will not always be outlined for parts of an exercise that have been covered in preceding modules. Likewise, steps that use basic concepts covered in earlier Pro Tools courses are not detailed in full. In completing the exercises, students should draw on their experience, and use the material available in this and other course books.

Exercise sections that include step-by-step instructions are marked as *Guided*. Other sections are marked *Challenge* and will set you on a task without any further instructions. In these sections, you should consult the preceding module for further guidance. Space is provided for you to note down the steps you took.

In some exercises, you have the option to build upon work carried out in previous exercises. Should you have any problems with re-using a session in an exercise, your instructor can help or provide you with a generic starting point for the exercise.

Compatible Hardware and Software

For complete, up-to-date information on compatible computers, computer peripherals, operating systems and software, refer to the compatibility section of Avid's website for the latest system requirements: *www.avid.com and click on the Support & Services link.*

Module 1 Preparing The Session

This module covers the steps required to prepare a session for composing and recording in a MIDI studio environment.

Objectives:

- Set a custom Song Start position

- Set advanced meter and click preferences

- Use MIDI Beat Clock

- Set a session's tempo to match an imported audio loop

- Set up your MIDI devices for use with Pro Tools

- Manipulate the audio from your MIDI devices within the Pro Tools mixer

- Import tracks and data from other Pro Tools sessions

Introduction

Modern music sessions often contain a mixture of audio recordings and MIDI data, performed with acoustic, electric, and software instruments. This course explores a range of contemporary production techniques for composing, recording, arranging and mixing music with Pro Tools. On completing this course, you will feel confident using Pro Tools as a music creation and production environment.

The main purpose of this module is to show you how to lay the foundations for a MIDI-based session, including how to configure your hardware MIDI devices and instruments to work with Pro Tools. The module covers techniques for preparing the musical framework of your session, configuring MIDI devices, routing MIDI sound sources into the Pro Tools mixer, and re-using data and tracks from previous sessions.

Song Start, Meter, and Tempo Revisited

As you have seen in previous courses, working within the context of a musical grid provides many advantages over using Pro Tools like a simple tape recorder. By setting an appropriate starting point, time signature, and tempo for your song, you can compose and record within a musical framework from the outset, greatly simplifying subsequent editing and arrangement tasks, and opening new creative avenues.

In this section, we discuss advanced concepts related to session preparation, such as altering the song start, setting up Meter using the Time Operations window, customizing the behavior of the Click track within the current time signature, and deriving a tempo from an existing recording.

Song Start

The Song Start is the position where the first beat of Bar 1 occurs in the Bars|Beats ruler; it is marked by the Song Start Marker, a red diamond marker in the Tempo track. The Song Start Marker is also a Tempo event that sets the tempo at the start of the song.

You may wish to move the song start so that Bar 1 does not occur immediately at the start of the session. Some common reasons for moving the Song Start include:

- To make a 'run-up,' allowing for easy manual pre-rolling.

- To ensure that notes played prior to 1|1|000 are accurately captured (MIDI notes played prior to 1|1|000 will not be recorded if the Song Start is at the far left of the timeline).

- To allow for breaths, pick-up notes, amp or fret noise, or even an audible count-off prior to Bar 1, beat 1.

- To allow for some introductory audio—for example an atmospheric sample or pad—you may want to specify exactly where bar 1 comes in for the main part of the song.

- In a music-for-picture scenario, to line up bar 1 against an appropriate place in the video track.

To move the Song Start Marker by dragging:

1 Display the Tempo and Bars:Beats rulers by choosing VIEW > RULERS > TEMPO and VIEW > RULERS > BARS:BEATS.

2 In the Tempo track, drag the Song Start Marker (red diamond) left or right.

Dragging the Song Start Marker

If Grid mode is enabled, the Song Start Marker will move in increments of the current grid value. Bar lines before bar 1 count backwards through zero and into negative values.

 This method of setting the song start will change the locations of any existing Bar|Beat-based memory locations, and any tick-based track content; however, it will not affect any absolute-based memory locations or sample-based track content.

An alternative method of setting the song start is to use the MOVE SONG START operation. This gives access to some extra options: you can choose how other material in the session is affected, and you can also offset the Song Start bar number if necessary.

To move the Song Start Marker using the Move Song Start operation:

1   Open the Move Song Start dialog box, using either of the following methods:

   –   Choose EVENT > TIME OPERATIONS > MOVE SONG START.

   – Or –

   –   Choose EVENT > TIME OPERATIONS > OPERATIONS WINDOW and select MOVE SONG START from the
       pop-up menu.

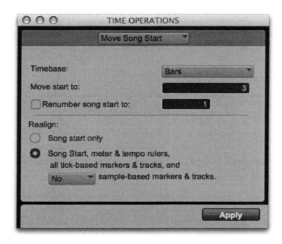

Move Song Start Page of the Time Operations window

2   Select a timebase to use from the TIMEBASE pop-up menu.

   –   This allows you to easily position the first bar at a timecode location.

3   Enter the position on the current timeline that you wish to apply for the song start in the MOVE START
   TO field. By default this will display the current position of the edit cursor, allowing you to set the
   start time visually in the time ruler before you open the Move Song Start window.

4   If desired, use the RENUMBER SONG START TO option to change which bar the Song Start Marker aligns
   to in the Bars:Beats ruler (default is bar 1, or the last used value).

5   Select from the options listed under MOVE to choose whether any existing ruler events and track
   contents are shifted with the Song Start. To move all session content, click the second radio button
   and select ALL from the pop-up menu.

Meter

In a new Pro Tools session, the meter defaults to 4/4. If you intend to work with the grid or record with a click, you need to set the meter to match your song. If a session's meter does not match the music you are recording, the accented clicks will not line up with what you are playing, and, as a result, the recorded material may not align correctly with the bars and beats in the Edit window.

Inserting Meter Events

Meter events can be inserted at the beginning of a session to replace the default meter, and they can be inserted anywhere within the session to create additional meter changes.

In the Pro Tools 110 course, you learned how to add meter events using the following methods:

- Clicking the ADD METER CHANGE button ("+" symbol) at the left of the Meter ruler.
- Double-clicking the CURRENT METER button in the Transport window.
- CONTROL-CLICKING (Mac) or START-CLICKING (Windows) in the Meter ruler.

Each of these actions will open the METER CHANGE window, where you can enter the location and meter for the event.

Another option for creating meter events is to use the TIME OPERATIONS window. This window provides advanced options that are not available in the Meter Change window.

To insert a meter event using the Time Operations window:

1   Do one of the following:

  − Choose EVENT > TIME OPERATIONS > CHANGE METER.

    − Or −

  − Choose EVENT > TIME OPERATIONS > OPERATIONS WINDOW and select the CHANGE METER page from the pop-up menu.

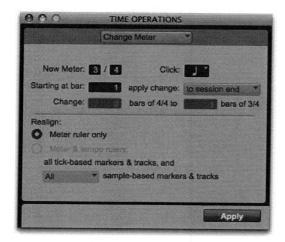

Change Meter page of the Time Operations window

2   In the Change Meter page, enter the new meter, and select a note value for the number of clicks to sound in each measure.

3   On the next line, enter the starting bar number, and select an option for the duration from the pop-up menu. The available choices include:

  – To selected range

  – To session end

  – Until next bar

4   If applying the change to a range, enter the number of bars to affect (in the original meter) in the CHANGE field; the TO field will calculate an equivalent range, using the nearest whole number of bars in the new meter.

5   Select the desired REALIGN options to specify whether the change affects the Meter ruler only, the Meter and tempo rulers and tick-based markers and tracks only, or all tick-based and sample-based markers, rulers, and tracks.

6   Click APPLY to insert the new meter event. The new meter event is inserted and appears in the Meter ruler.

 If a meter change is applied to a selected range that is not cleanly divisible by the new meter, time will be inserted in the affected rulers and tracks to maintain a whole number of bars (i.e. to avoid the creation of partial bars).

You can use the Change Meter page of the Time Operations window to add or cut time in your session as you add meter change events. By applying meter changes to a selected range and using a TO value that is larger or smaller than the equivalent CHANGE value, you can insert or remove time on the rulers, markers, and tracks selected by the REALIGN options.

 The Time Operations window also has pages for INSERT TIME and CUT TIME. These operations are discussed in Module 7.

Meter and the Click

As you'd expect, the behavior of the Click Track is set by the Meter and Tempo at each point in the song. In many cases, especially with simple meters, this will result in an appropriate click to perform to. However, with more complex meters, and in polyrhythmic compositions (where different players are playing in different meters), the default click may not be the best choice.

Adjusting the Click for a Meter

Both the simple Meter Change window, and the Time Operations Change Meter dialog allow you to adjust the click by specifying the length of a beat independently of the meter's native beat length. By default, the click plays quarter-notes. So, for example, if you if set the meter to 12/8 the click will still play quarter notes, despite the fact that the desired click for this meter is often a dotted quarter note.

To change the beat reference for the Click:

1   Create a new meter change event by any method, or open an existing one for editing by double-clicking the meter event in the meter ruler.

2   In the 'Click' pop-up menu, choose a note length (as shown below).

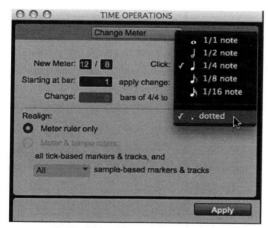

Changing the beat reference for the Click

In the example of a 12/8 meter, you might choose to change the Click setting to a dotted quarter note, resulting in four evenly-spaced clicks. The choice you make is a matter of preference for the performer, and will depend on the song, the tempo, and the meter.

An Example: "Everybody Hurts" by REM

"Everybody Hurts" by REM is a well known example of a song written in 12/8 time (four groups of three eighth notes in each bar). It's also a great example of a situation where adjusting the click is likely to yield a more natural guide when recording. The song is roughly 100 bpm in tempo (at quarter-note resolution), but to the listener the four groups of three eighth notes per measure feel more like about 65 bpm.

In Pro Tools, if you set up 12/8 time at 100 bpm, the Click Track (defaulting to quarter-notes) yields six clicks per bar, which doesn't work well as a click for this song. A slightly better result is attained by changing the Click to eighth notes, resulting in 12 clicks per bar. While this is usable, it is quite fast and intrusive. It would be preferable to have the click count the four beats per measure that one naturally taps with a foot when listening to the song. This is achieved by setting the Click to dotted quarter-notes.

Matching Session Tempo to an Audio Loop

You have already learned how to set the default tempo for your session (PT101), and how to create additional tempo changes (PT110). You have also learned how to conform audio loops to the tempo of the session using Elastic Audio. In this section, you will learn how to take the opposite approach: setting the tempo of the session to match an existing audio loop.

It's quite common for a composition to start from a basic idea that's a few bars long. This could be a guitar riff, chord progression, or drum pattern that was recorded without a click track as a starting point. It could also be an imported audio loop that will be the inspiration for the session. Either way, once this musical keystone has been imported or recorded into your session, you may want to apply its tempo to the session.

The Event menu command IDENTIFY BEAT lets you tell Pro Tools how long a loop is in bars (based on the performance) and have Pro Tools realign the Bar|Beat grid accordingly. The tempo ruler is updated automatically to reflect the changes.

To use the Identify Beat command to match the session tempo to an audio loop:

1   Import or record a loop or pattern, and edit it as needed to accurately represent a whole number of bars/beats.

2   Place the pattern at the desired position on a track.

– In the following example, a 2-bar loop has been placed at Bar 1. Since the loop does not end on a bar, it is clearly not at the same tempo as the session.

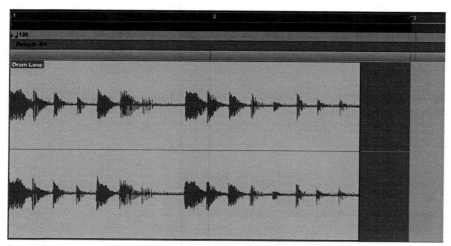

A two-bar loop that is faster than the session tempo

3   Select the loop using the GRABBER tool.

4   Choose EVENT > IDENTIFY BEAT, or press COMMAND+I (Mac) or CTRL+I (Windows). The Add Bar|Beat Markers dialog box will open

 The Conductor Track/Tempo Ruler must be enabled (in the Edit or Transport window) in order for the Identify Beat function to be available. In manual tempo mode (with the Conductor disabled), the Identify Beat function will be grayed out in the Event menu.

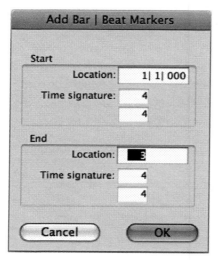

The Add Bar|Beat Markers dialog box

5   In the dialog box, enter the locations of the start and end of your selection. In this case the loop is 2 bars long and begins on bar 1 beat 1, so you would enter 1|1|000 for the start location and 3|1|000 for the end location.

6   If needed, adjust the Time signatures for the start and/or end locations to match the meter of the loop.

7   Click OK. The new tempo will be calculated, and the necessary Bar|Beat markers and meter events will be inserted. Any existing tempo and meter events residing within the selection will be deleted.

 The properties of Bar|Beat markers are discussed in more detail in Module 6 of this book.

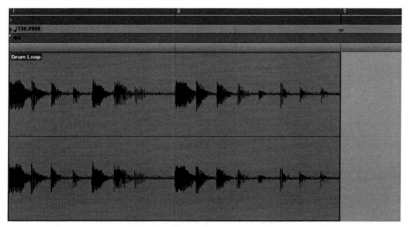

The new tempo will continue up to any subsequent tempo events in the session. In a new session, there will be no other beat markers, so the new tempo will extend throughout the session.

Interacting with External MIDI Devices

Although much composition work can be completed within the Pro Tools environment using Virtual Instrument plug-ins, the ability to work with hardware MIDI devices remains an essential studio skill. In this section you will learn how to send Program Change messages to MIDI instruments to recall settings, and use MIDI Beat Clock to synchronize tempo and song position. You will also review ways to monitor and record the audio signals from your MIDI instruments with Pro Tools.

 Refer to the Pro Tools 110 book for a description of how to connect and config-ure MIDI between instruments and Pro Tools. MIDI connections can be viewed and edited by choosing SETUP > MIDI > MIDI STUDIO *in Pro Tools.*

Using MIDI Beat Clock

MIDI Beat Clock is a synchronization signal that contains timing pulses based on tempo (at a rate of 24 pulses per quarter-note). Many MIDI devices such as drum machines, hardware sequencers, and modulation sources within synths can be synchronized to MIDI Beat Clock. Pro Tools can generate MIDI Beat Clock and send it to these devices, and they will play back in time with the session's tempo. The MIDI Beat Clock sent by Pro Tools also contains Song Position Pointers, allowing devices to sync to the correct position in the timeline as well as play in time. Many plug-ins and virtual instruments also support MIDI Beat Clock and are configured in the same way.

To transmit MIDI Beat Clock:

1   Choose SETUP > MIDI > MIDI BEAT CLOCK. The MIDI Beat Clock dialog box will open.

2   At the top of the dialog box, verify that the option to Enable MIDI Beat Clock is selected.

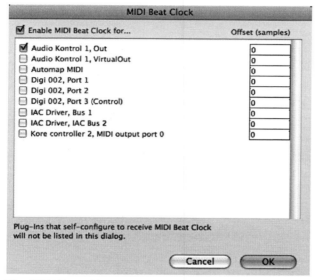

The MIDI Beat Clock dialog box

3   Select the devices, MIDI ports, and/or plug-ins that you want to send MIDI Beat Clock to.

 Many plug-ins and plug-in virtual instruments are automatically configured to receive beat clock in the background and are not listed in the MIDI Beat Clock window. Plug-ins that do not have this feature are listed and must be selected in order to receive Beat Clock.

4   Click OK to close the dialog box.

Routing Audio from MIDI Instruments through Pro Tools

Several options exist for routing the audio outputs of your external MIDI devices. Though you might simply monitor your MIDI instruments through an external mixer, far more flexibility is gained by routing audio through the Pro Tools mixer. Some advantages of routing through Pro Tools include the following:

- You can record your MIDI performances as audio at any time.
- All your audio signals are managed in a single integrated environment.
- You can use plug-ins to process audio from your MIDI instruments.
- You can use Pro Tools automation in the mixer channels.
- Your mixer settings will be stored and recalled as part of the session.

Connecting Audio

Audio from external MIDI devices can be connected to any analog input on a Pro Tools interface, but the level of the signal must be taken into consideration. MIDI instruments generally have audio outputs that use the -10dBV level standard, which HD-series interfaces will be able to receive directly when the correct input options are chosen. Alternatively, the device's output can be routed through an external mixer or preamp (such as the Digidesign PRE) to provide input gain control.

Connecting MIDI instruments Directly to an HD Series Interface

HD OMNI and HD I/O--The HD OMNI and HD I/O can be configured for +4 or -10 level inputs for each channel. When connecting your MIDI devices, you need to ensure that the inputs you are using are configured for the right reference level, typically -10dBV. You can select the reference level for each channel in the Analog In page of the Hardware Setup dialog box (Setup>Hardware) for each interface.

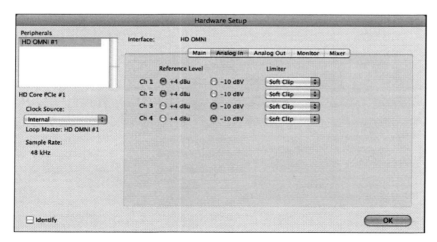

HD OMNI analog input options

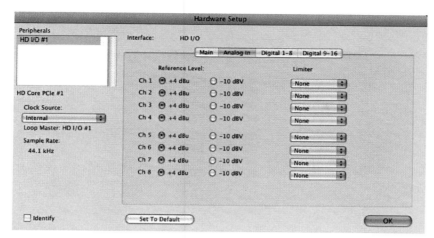

HD I/O analog input options

192 I/O--The 192 I/O features separate connectors for +4 and -10 level inputs. When connecting MIDI devices, you need to select inputs of the correct type, typically the -10dBV inputs. You must also select the correct reference level for the channels you are using in the Hardware Setup dialog box.

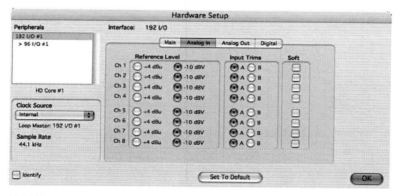

192 I/O Input Options

96 I/O--The 96 I/O has 8 analog inputs via 1/4-inch TRS connectors. Your instruments can be connected via balanced or unbalanced jack cables. Once connected, you use the Hardware Setup dialog box to switch the inputs to the correct operating level settings (+4 or -10), similar to the HD OMNI and HD I/O.

96i I/O--The 96i I/O is designed for connecting line-level sources directly to Pro Tools and has 16 1/4-inch TRS analog inputs. The 96i includes Sensitivity Level sliders for Inputs 1-4 in the Hardware Setup dialog box, allowing you to set an input level between -12dBV and +4dBu. Inputs 5-16 can be switched between -8dBV and +4dBu.

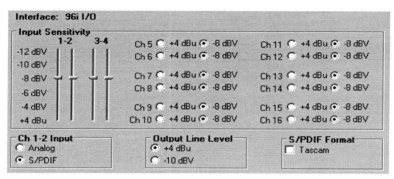

96i Hardware Setup options

Connecting MIDI Devices to Pro Tools via a Mixer or Preamp

If the output level of a MIDI instrument is too low to get an acceptable input level into Pro Tools, then you can connect via an external mixer or preamp. If you are using an Avid PRE, you should choose Line as the input source type.

Routing Audio through an Instrument Track

Although you can control a MIDI device from a MIDI track and monitor the audio via an Aux Input track, you will probably find it easier to use an Instrument Track to achieve the same functionality in a single mixer channel. Instrument Tracks combine the features of MIDI and Aux Input tracks, so you can use them to route and record MIDI for a device, while simultaneously monitoring and routing audio from that instrument.

To route audio from an external MIDI device using an Instrument Track:

1   Create a new mono or stereo Instrument Track by choosing TRACK > NEW or pressing COMMAND+SHIFT+N (Mac) or CTRL+SHIFT+N (Windows).

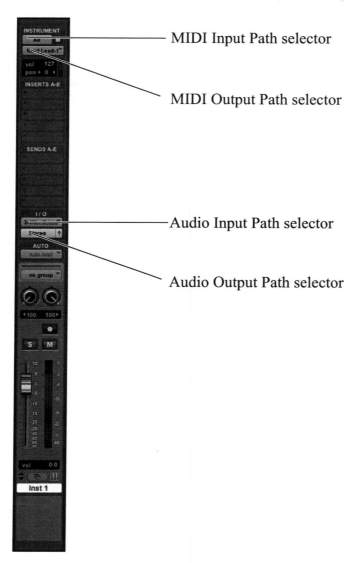

MIDI Input Path selector

MIDI Output Path selector

Audio Input Path selector

Audio Output Path selector

2   Use the MIDI Input Path selector to specify the port and channel to use to receive data from your MIDI instrument, as needed. If left to its default (ALL), the track will receive MIDI input from all channels on all available MIDI ports.

3   Use the MIDI Output Path selector to select the MIDI instrument that you want to send MIDI signals to during playback. In this scenario, you would select the same instrument you are using to send MIDI data to Pro Tools.

4   Select the audio input you've connected your instrument to from the Audio Input Path selector.

5   Route the audio output of the track as required, using the Audio Output Path selector.

Recording to an Audio Track

After a MIDI performance has been recorded and edited, you may want to record the audio output of the instrument. To do this, the audio signal from the Instrument Track must be routed to an available Audio track.

To route the audio output of an Instrument Track to an audio track:

1   Set the Audio Output Path of the Instrument track to an available mono or stereo bus (as appropriate).

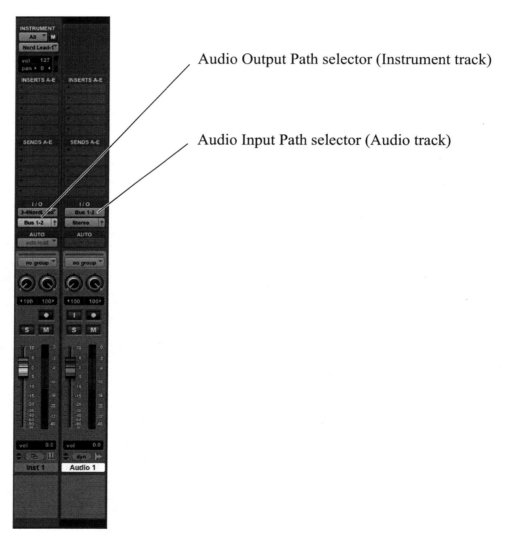

Audio Output Path selector (Instrument track)

Audio Input Path selector (Audio track)

2   Set the Audio track's Input Path selector to the same internal bus as the Output of the Instrument track.

3   Record-enable the Audio track and begin recording.

4   After recording is complete, select the Instrument track and choose TRACK > MAKE INACTIVE.

5   [Optional] Hide the Instrument track.

 You can also hide and deactivate a track with one command: RIGHT-CLICK *on the track name and choose* HIDE AND MAKE INACTIVE *from the pop-up menu.*

You can deactivate and hide the Instrument Track because you now have the part printed as audio. However, all the MIDI and Audio routing will remain intact if future MIDI editing or preset/patch changes are required.

Recording Pre or Post Plug-ins

Using the above method will record the results of any plug-ins on the Instrument Track. If you wish to record only the dry signal, and continue to use the plug-ins on the Audio Track, simply drag-and-drop the plug-ins from the Instrument Track to the Audio Track before recording. In fact, if you are not recording the result of plug-ins or automation on the Instrument Track, you can simply set the Input of the Audio Track to receive the external instrument's signal directly, and bypass any internal bussing.

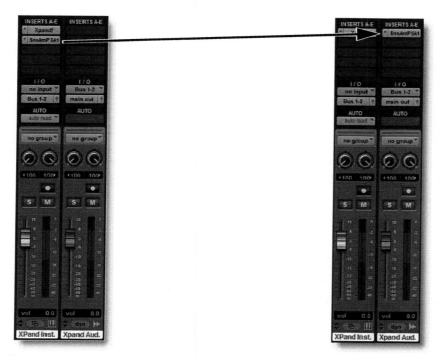

Recording setup including the SansAmp plug-in (left) and excluding the SansAmp plug-in (right)

Importing Data from Other Sessions

Re-using Tracks

As you have learned in previous courses, when you start a new session from the Quick Start dialog box, the session can be blank, or it can be built from a template containing pre-determined tracks. You can of course create your own Quick Start templates; a detailed exploration of creating templates suited to your projects can be found in the Pro Tools 310M course.

However, in many real-world situations a faster and more flexible approach is to import and re-use tracks from earlier projects. Here are some examples where importing tracks may be advantageous:

- In a different song/session, you've set up a great synth bass sound comprising a track with a virtual instrument such as Hybrid, followed by specific processing, such as a compressor and a chorus plug-in. Now you want to use that same configuration in the current session without having to set everything up from scratch.

- You are recording several songs for a band's album. Many songs have elements in common, for example: a guitar with a particular amp simulator plug-in setting or vocals routed through a favorite hardware insert. When you start each new song, you want to bring in and re-use some of the tracks that you set up in the previous sessions, saving time and helping maintain a consistent sound for the album.

- You have a complex mixer configuration, such as an instance of the Structure plug-in that is bussing multiple audio channels to other tracks. This would be a time-consuming configuration to set up more than once.

Importing tracks saves you time because you can bring them in with all their input, output, plug-in, and MIDI assignments in place.

As you saw in the Pro Tools 110 course, the Import Session Data dialog box gives you a large number of options (these options are even more extensive with a Pro Tools | HD system). The Import Session Data enables you to import the contents of tracks to existing tracks in your current session, and to pick and choose from various data types to import. In the Pro Tools 110 course, you used the Import Session Data feature to import tracks with audio. In this section, we will instead import blank tracks to use in a new composition.

To import track templates from another session:

1 Choose FILE > IMPORT > SESSION DATA, or press OPTION+SHIFT+I (Mac) or ALT+SHIFT+I (Windows). An OPEN dialog box will appear.

2 Navigate to and select the session file that contains your track templates. Click OPEN.

   – The Import Session Data dialog box will appear.

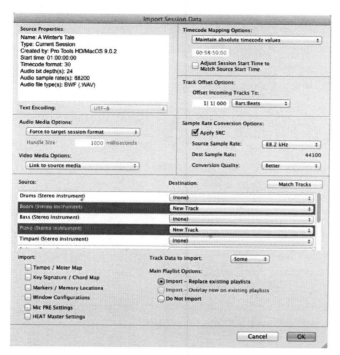

3 Select the tracks that you wish to import, leaving the Destination pop-up menu set to New Track. The following options are available when making selections:

   – Tracks can be selected for importing by clicking on them individually. Clicking subsequent tracks does not de-select previous ones.

   – Selected tracks can be de-selected by clicking on them a second time.

   – Multiple adjacent tracks can be selected by Shift-clicking.

   – All tracks can be selected by pressing COMMAND+A (Mac) or CTRL+A (Windows), or by holding the Option (Mac) or Alt (Windows) key when selecting a single track.

   In addition to tracks and their attributes, you can also import other reusable features from a session with the Import Session Data dialog box. The Session Data To Import pop-up menu lets you choose from a list of data associated with the tracks that you import. The available options include things like alternate playlists, automation playlists, voice assignments, and Mix and Edit Group assignments.

4   After selecting the desired tracks, choose the aspects of the tracks that you wish to bring into your
session from the SESSION DATA TO IMPORT pop-up menu.

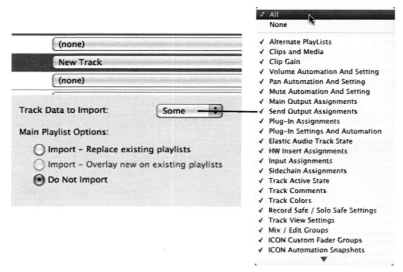

Use this pop-up to check/uncheck items one at a time until you have the combination of data
you require. You may find it quickest to choose None first, then add any track assignments that
you wish to import (if importing just a few), or choose All first, then remove any track
assignments that you don't wish to import (if importing many).

Common choices could include Input and Output assignments, Send assignments, Plug-in
assignments (e.g. for virtual instruments), and Mix/Edit groups.

5   From the Main Playlist Options choose DO NOT IMPORT. This will strip out the audio and MIDI contents
of the tracks that you import.

6   Click OK to import the selected tracks.

Importing Other Reusable Features

The IMPORT section of the Import Session Data dialog box allows you to selectively import any of the following features from another session:

- The Tempo/Meter map. (NOTE: Importing tempo and meter maps will overwrite the existing tempo and meter maps of your session.)

- The Key Signature /Chord map. (NOTE: Importing Key Signature and Chord maps will overwrite the existing Key Signature and Chord maps of your session.)

- Markers/MemoryLocations

- Window Configurations

- Mic PRE settings (if available)

- HEAT Master Settings (if available)

The markers/memory locations option can be especially useful if you use memory locations to store favorite zoom, window configuration, and track view settings (see Module 8).

To import Markers/Memory Locations, Window Configurations, or other options:

1   Choose FILE > IMPORT > SESSION DATA.

2   Select the session you wish to import from.

3   Check the desired options, such as MARKERS/MEMORY LOCATIONS and/or WINDOW CONFIGURATIONS, in the IMPORT section at the bottom of the Import Session Data dialog box.

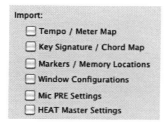

Import section of the Import Session Data dialog box

4   Click OK to import the selected items.

 Recalling an imported Memory Location that includes Track Show/Hide properties will hide all tracks in your session other than those imported concurrently with the Memory Location.

Review Questions

1   Describe two ways to change a song's start time. (See "Song Start" on page 2.)

2   True or False: Manually dragging the session Song Start Marker to a new location will affect the timing of all data and clips on both tick-based and sample-based tracks. (See "Song Start" on page 2.)

3   What is the default meter applied to Pro Tools sessions? (See "Meter" on page 5.)

4   When might you want to use the Time Operations window rather than the Meter Change window to insert a meter change? (See "Inserting Meter Events" on page 5.)

5   What modifier would you hold to add a Meter Change by clicking on the Meter ruler? (See "Inserting Meter Events" on page 5.)

6   What is the purpose of the Identify Beat command? (See "Matching Session Tempo to an Audio Loop" on page 8.)

7   What condition would cause the Identify Beat command to be grayed out in the Event menu? (See "Matching Session Tempo to an Audio Loop" on page 8.)

8   What is MIDI Beat Clock? How many pulses does it provide per quarter note? (See "Using MIDI Beat Clock" on page 11.)

9   What are some advantages of routing the audio from your hardware MIDI instruments through Pro Tools? (See "Routing Audio from MIDI Instruments through Pro Tools" on page 12.)

10   How would you import Mix and Edit Groups to use with Track Templates? (See "Importing Other Reusable Features" on page 21.)

Exercise 1 Session Preparation & Import

In this exercise you will prepare a session using the techniques from Module 1.

Objectives:

- Create a new session from a Template
- Set the Song Start point
- Import template tracks from an existing session
- Set the song's default tempo to match an imported loop

Approximate Completion Time: 15-20 minutes.

Start a New Session

Task	Direction	Steps Used to Achieve Task
1	Create a new session from the template called 210M Template.ptxt from the location specified by your instructor (such as Audio Drive: 210M PT10 Class Files: 210M PT10 Exercise 1). Name the new session <your initials> 210M Exercise 1.	

Set the Song Start Time [Challenge]

Task	Direction	Steps Used to Achieve Task
1	Adjust the Song Start to provide a 2-bar run-up before Bar 1.	
	Use the first method discussed in Module 1 (dragging the Song Start Marker).	
	When you've finished, the session should start at Bar -1 (negative 1).	

Import Track Data from a Previous Session [Challenge]

In this section you will use the Import Session Data command to re-use tracks and settings from a previous session.

Task	Direction	Steps Used to Achieve Task
1	Import drum recording tracks from an earlier session.	

The session you will import tracks from is called "210M Previous Session." Your instructor will provide the location (such as Audio Drive: 210M PT10 Class Files: 210M PT10 Exercise 1: 210M Previous Session.ptx).

Import the following tracks as new tracks:

Kick

Snare Top

Snare Bottom

Hi Hat

Overheads

Drum Submix

Do not import the audio and playlists. Only import the following:

Main Output Assignments

Send Output Assignments

Plug-In Assignments

Plug-In Settings and Automation

Input Assignments

Mix/Edit Groups

```
         All
         None

         Alternate PlayLists
         Clips and Media
         Clip Gain
         Volume Automation And Setting
         Pan Automation And Setting
         Mute Automation And Setting
    ✓    Main Output Assignments
    ✓    Send Output Assignments
    ✓    Plug-In Assignments
    ✓    Plug-In Settings And Automation
         Elastic Audio Track State
         HW Insert Assignments
    ✓    Input Assignments
         Sidechain Assignments
         Track Active State
         Track Comments
         Track Colors
         Record Safe / Solo Safe Settings
         Track View Settings
    ✓    Mix / Edit Groups
         ICON Custom Fader Groups
         ICON Automation Snapshots
         HEAT Switch Settings
```

Task	Direction	Steps Used to Achieve Task
2	Import the track Hybrid Bass directly to the track in your template session called Synth Bass.	

The only Track Data to import should be Plug-in Assignments and Plug-In Settings and Automation. This will import the Hybrid plug-in, along with the Plug-in settings appropriate for this track.

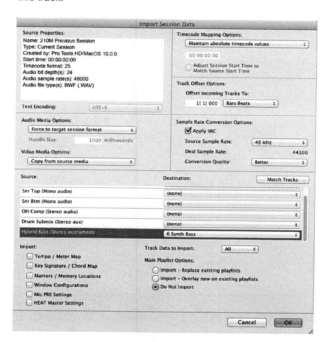

Derive tempo from an audio loop [Challenge]

Task	Direction	Steps Used to Achieve Task
1	Import a loop to a new track and set the session's tempo to match it.	

Import a loop to a new track and set the session's tempo to match it.

The loop to import is called "Groove.wav" and can be found in the 210M PT10 Exercise 1 folder in the location specified by your instructor.

Use the Identify Beat command to create a Bar|Beat marker, as described in Module 1.

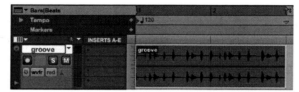

Save and close your session.

That concludes this exercise.

Module 2   Tracking and Overdubbing

This module covers key recording techniques for the professional studio engineer or recording musician. Using the techniques described in this module, students will be able to accommodate a variety of different recording styles, helping to bring out the best performance of the performing musicians.

Objectives:
- Work in Dynamic Transport mode
- Utilize advanced MIDI recording options
- Use QuickPunch and TrackPunch record modes
- Understand and use input monitoring modes
- Record and "comp" multiple takes

Introduction

This module covers a number of recording techniques that are essential in a professional music environment. First, you'll learn an important way of managing playback position and timeline selections. You will then learn how to drop in and overdub recordings on-the-fly, manage the routing of monitoring and playback signals, and finally to compile a performance from multiple takes.

Working in Dynamic Transport Mode

In previous courses you have examined two different ways to manage the playback position in the Pro Tools timeline: using linked or unlinked Timeline and Edit selections. By default, LINK TIMELINE AND EDIT SELECTION mode is on, so the playback position is always tied (either directly or with a pre-roll) to the current Edit selection in the Edit window. As you learned, it can be advantageous to disable LINK TIMELINE AND EDIT SELECTION mode so that you can define a playback range that persists when you perform an edit.

Dynamic Transport mode goes one step further, affording you complete control over the current playback position without disturbing either the Edit or Timeline selections. Using Dynamic Transport mode, you can set up a timeline range or loop and specify the exact point (inside or outside of the loop) where playback begins. This playback point can be moved at any time, including during playback. Dynamic Transport mode allows you to manage timeline and transport operations in a similar way to many MIDI sequencer applications, and it is especially useful when tracking a song in sections or when editing loops.

Pro Tools provides several methods for activating and deactivating Dynamic Transport mode.

To activate Dynamic Transport mode, do one of the following:

- Select OPTIONS > DYNAMIC TRANSPORT.

- Press CONTROL+COMMAND+P (Mac) or CTRL+START+P (Windows).

- Right-click on the PLAY button in the Transport window or the Edit window and select DYNAMIC TRANSPORT from the pop-up menu.

  The Main Timebase ruler will expand to double-height, and the Play Start Marker will display at the start of the Timeline selection.

To deactivate Dynamic Transport mode:

• Repeat any of the above actions.

When you enable Dynamic Transport mode, the Main Timebase ruler will expand to double-height. The top half of the ruler will display the Timeline Selection Markers (blue up and down arrows), while the bottom half displays the Play Start Marker (blue Play triangle).

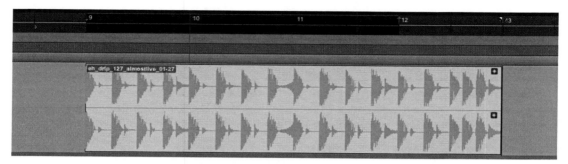

Double-height Timebase ruler in Dynamic Transport mode

About the Play Start Marker

The Play Start Marker determines where playback will start when the Pro Tools Transport is engaged. You can position the Play Start Marker independently of the Timeline selection, so playback can begin from any point before the selection, within the selection, or after the selection. You can also reposition the Play Start Marker during playback, and playback will continue from the new location.

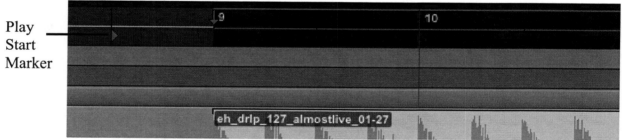

Play Start Marker in the Main Timebase ruler

To reposition the Play Start Marker, do one of the following:

• With any Edit tool selected, click and drag on the Play Start Marker.

• With any Edit tool selected, click anywhere in the Play Start Marker strip. The Play Start Marker will jump to the clicked location.

• Click the Fast Forward or Rewind buttons in the Transport window or Edit window to relocate the Play Start Marker by the standard Fast Forward and Rewind increment amount. Click and hold the Fast Forward or Rewind buttons to move rapidly forward or backward.

During playback, you can click anywhere in the Play Start marker strip to move the Play Start Marker and continue playback. When stopped, you can double-click anywhere in the Play Start marker strip to move the Play Start Marker to that location and start playback.

Dynamic Transport and Timeline/Edit Selections

Selecting Dynamic Transport mode will automatically disable the Link Timeline and Edit Selection option. If desired, you can enable Link Timeline and Edit Selection with Dynamic Transport mode active. When you deactivate Dynamic Transport mode, the Link Timeline and Edit Selection option will return to its previous setting (for example, whatever state it was in prior to activating Dynamic Transport).

Dynamic Transport and Loop Playback

Activating Dynamic Transport mode will automatically enable Loop Playback mode, if not already active. If desired, you can disable Loop Playback mode while Dynamic Transport mode is active. When you deactivate Dynamic Transport mode, Loop Playback mode will return to its previous setting (for example, whatever state it was in prior to activating Dynamic Transport).

Moving the Timeline Selection

You can use all the usual selection techniques to make and modify Timeline and Edit selections while Dynamic Transport is active. You can also grab the entire timeline selection and move it to another location, keeping the current selection's length (by holding the Option (Mac) or Alt (Windows) key while moving a Timeline Selection point). This can be very useful when working on a song in sections, such as 8 bars at a time.

Dynamic Transport Preferences

Depending on your settings, you may find that the Play Start Marker will snap to the Timeline Selection In Point when you move the Timeline selection, make a new Timeline selection, or adjust the Timeline selection start location. You may also find that the Play Start Marker will move to the point in the Timeline where you stop playback. Both of these behaviors can be enabled/disabled through Preference settings.

To set the Play Start Marker behavior relative to the Timeline selection:

1   Choose Setup > Preferences.

2   Click the Operation tab.

3   Select/deselect Play Start Marker Follows Timeline Selection.

4   Click OK to close the Preferences window.

   – When deselected, the Play Start Marker will remain stationary while you create, move, or adjust your Timeline selection.

To set the Play Start Marker behavior relative to the playback stopping point:

1   Choose SETUP > PREFERENCES.

2   Click the OPERATION tab.

3   Select/deselect TIMELINE INSERTION/PLAY START MARKER FOLLOWS PLAYBACK.

 This can also be done directly from the Edit window by clicking the "Insertion Follows Playback" button.

4   Click OK to close the Preferences window.

   – When deselected, the Play Start Marker will remain stationary after playback stops, enabling you to audition from the same starting point repeatedly.

Tracking

The remainder of this module is dedicated to recording techniques, such as how to filter out unwanted MIDI data, how to perform punch-ins, how to manage your monitoring sources, and how to compile a 'best performance' from multiple takes.

Using the MIDI Input Filter

The MIDI Input Filter can be used to prevent specified MIDI messages from being recorded. For example, this function is commonly used to filter aftertouch from your controller keyboard.

The MIDI Input Filter can be set to record All messages, Only specified messages, or All Except specified messages. The default settings pass all MIDI messages through to be recorded except mono aftertouch and polyphonic aftertouch.

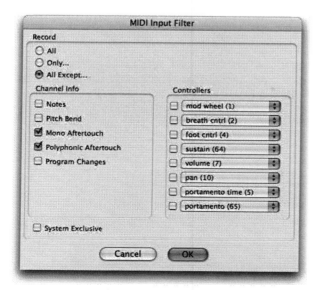

MIDI Input Filter dialog box

To filter out a specific type of MIDI data using the MIDI Input Filter settings:

1   Choose SETUP > MIDI > INPUT FILTER. The MIDI Input Filter dialog box will open.

2   Under RECORD, select the ALL EXCEPT option.

3   Select the options to exclude from recording; for example, to filter out only Pitch Bend messages, select PITCH BEND in the CHANNEL INFO section. Leave all other options deselected.

4   Click OK.

 When using the All Except option, the selected MIDI data type will not be recorded. Conversely, when using the Only option, the selected MIDI data type is the only data type that will be recorded.

Monitor Modes and TrackInput

During a recording session you often need to be able to switch between listening to the live signals from your instruments/mics and listening to what you've previously recorded. Pro Tools uses a single mixer channel for monitoring inputs and for playing back recorded material on each track, enabling you to be able to control which of these two sources is being monitored.

Auto Input Monitoring

By default all Audio Tracks in Pro Tools HD are in Auto Input Monitoring mode. In this mode, you hear the live inputs on record-enabled tracks whenever Pro Tools is stopped or is recording. However, you hear the recorded material from the track during playback. When using QuickPunch, the monitor source for the track will switch on-the-fly as you punch in and out.

Input Only Monitoring

Tracks that are in Input Only Monitoring mode will always pass through their live input, and anything recorded to the track will not be heard. Any Audio Track can be switched into Input Only mode by pressing its TrackInput button. Input Only Monitoring is active when the TrackInput button is lit.

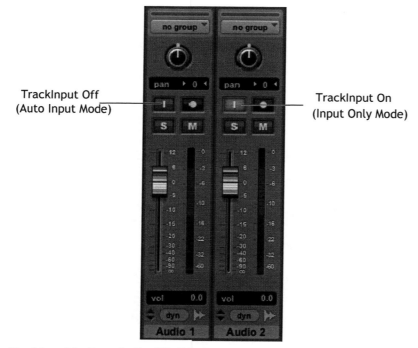

TrackInput Off (Auto Input Mode) TrackInput On (Input Only Mode)

TrackInput buttons in the Mix Window

The TrackInput buttons can toggle individual audio tracks between Auto Input and Input Only monitoring modes at any time, including during playback or recording. When a track's TrackInput button is on (lit green), the track is in Input Only mode, and you will hear the live input. When the TrackInput button is off, the track is in Auto Input mode; you will hear the live input during recording (or record enable) and the recorded material during playback.

In many cases Auto Input mode is the preferred mode, as it routes the monitoring source you are likely to require at any time in typical recording workflows. However, the TrackInput buttons become useful in certain situations:

- By enabling Input Only mode, you can monitor the input of any track during playback without it being record-enabled, allowing you to try out new ideas and alternatives for a recorded track.

- You may have instruments or mic sources that you want to monitor while recording other sources. By using an Audio tracks in Input mode, you have more flexibility than if you used Aux Inputs, because you can switch to recording those sources at any time on the same track without bussing.

- During a punch-in pass, the musician may prefer to hear him/herself prior to the punch point, allowing them to warm up and perform naturally.

- You can simulate and rehearse punch-ins without actually recording anything by playing back a track with TrackInput off, then switching it to Input Only mode at the proposed punch-in point. This working method is similar to using a multitrack recorder with Rehearse Mode functionality.

 Remember that Pro Tools punches non-destructively, so you may prefer to always record all experiments and "rehearsals" in case they are particularly good takes. You can always hit UNDO *for the takes you don't want to keep.*

To toggle the monitoring mode of audio tracks, do one of the following:

- To toggle individual tracks, click the TrackInput button for each track you want to toggle. The TrackInput button will light green when enabled.

- To toggle all tracks in the session, OPTION-CLICK (Mac) or ALT-CLICK (Windows) on a TrackInput button. All the TrackInput buttons will toggle green on/off.

- To toggle all selected tracks in the session, OPTION+SHIFT-CLICK (Mac) or ALT+SHIFT-CLICK (Windows) on a selected track's TrackInput button. All the TrackInput buttons for the selected tracks will toggle green on/off.

- To toggle all tracks that contain an Edit selection or Play Start Marker, press SHIFT+I.

To change the monitoring mode of all record-enabled tracks, do one of the following:

- To change all record-enabled tracks to Input Only monitoring mode, choose TRACK > SET RECORD TRACKS TO INPUT ONLY.

- To change all record-enabled tracks to Auto Input monitoring mode, choose TRACK > SET RECORD TRACKS TO AUTO INPUT.

- To toggle the monitoring mode of all record-enabled tracks between Input Only monitoring mode and Auto Input monitoring mode, press OPTION+K (Mac) or ALT+K (Windows).

Monitoring Mode Preferences

The OPERATION page of the Pro Tools Preferences dialog box has two user preferences that affect monitoring mode behavior.

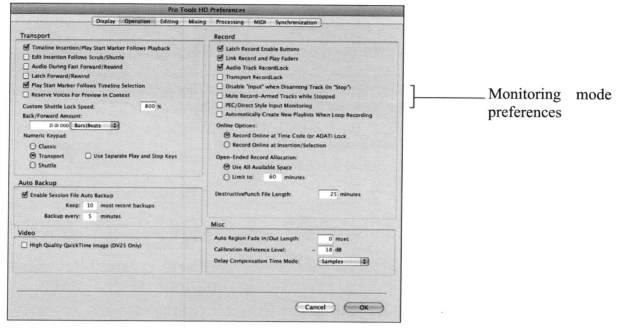

Monitoring mode preferences

Monitoring mode preference settings

- Disable "Input" When Disarming Track (In "Stop")—When enabled, this preference cancels TrackInput on audio tracks whenever they are taken out of record-enable mode and switches the tracks Auto Input mode. When disabled, audio tracks will remain in TrackInput mode until explicitly switched to Auto Input monitoring.

 Choosing this option will often result in a faster workflow for writing/recording sessions, allowing you to listen to recorded material after it has been recorded.

- Mute Record-Armed Tracks while Stopped—When enabled, this preference mutes live input on tracks that are record-enabled (and in Auto Input mode) while the Transport is stopped. This is useful when recording foley or in other situations where the mics are being handled or repositioned between record takes. (Input can still be monitored while stopped using the TrackInput button, e.g., for a listen mic.) When not enabled, Pro Tools monitors live input on tracks that are record-enabled.

 MUTE RECORD-ARMED TRACKS WHILE STOPPED *is disabled by default. This is the "classic" Pro Tools behavior, and it is usually preferable so that artists can still hear themselves when Pro Tools is stopped.*

QuickPunch and TrackPunch

Recording during a creative recording session needs to be fast and flexible. You (or your clients) may be experimenting with ideas, and you will want to get parts down quickly and make speedy changes, corrections, and overdubs. You may not have time to stop, set a pre-roll, and make a selection for recording.

QuickPunch is a Pro Tools recording mode that lets you instantaneously punch in (initiate recording) on any record-enabled audio tracks during playback and then punch out (exit recording), without ever stopping playback. This mode provides up to 200 running punches per record take. When QuickPunch mode is active, pressing Record on the Pro Tools Transport will begin recording into the timeline on all record-enabled tracks. When you record using QuickPunch, the newly recorded material is recorded into new clips and audio files.

Using QuickPunch

If you intend to punch into record during playback, you must first enable QuickPunch mode. This mode provides up to 200 running punches per record take.

To start and stop recording on the fly using QuickPunch:

1   Enable QuickPunch using any one of the following methods:

  – Choose OPTIONS > QUICKPUNCH.

  – Press the QUICKPUNCH button on your Control Surface.

  – Right-click on the RECORD button and choose QuickPunch.

  – Press [6] on the numeric keypad if it's in Transport Mode.

  The Record button will display a letter P when QuickPunch mode is active.

QuickPunch enabled

2   Record-enable the tracks you want to record to. The tracks' Record Enable buttons will flash red.

3   Begin playback.

4   When you want to punch in, initiate recording using any of the normal methods (Record button on your Control Surface, keyboard, Transport window, etc.). The Track Record Enable buttons will be lit solidly red during recording.

5   When you want to punch out, press/click a RECORD button again.

  – Pro Tools will continue playing back with recording suspended (flashing Record Enable button).

6   To perform additional punch-ins, click the RECORD button at subsequent punch-in and punch-out points (up to 200 running punches per record take). Each punch is recorded as a separate clip in the same new sound file.

7 When finished, stop playback and disable recording on your tracks, as needed.

 When a track is record-enabled, Pro Tools automatically suspends delay compensation for that track to ensure low-latency monitoring.

 An additional free voice must be held in reserve for each record-enabled channel when using QuickPunch.

Setting QuickPunch/TrackPunch Crossfade Preferences

You can choose to have Pro Tools automatically create crossfades whenever you punch in and out to avoid clicks or obvious punch-in transitions. To enable crossfades, choose SETUP > PREFERENCES and select the EDITING tab. Under the FADES section, set a value for QuickPunch/TrackPunch crossfade length. You can choose a length between 0 and 1000ms, with 0 switching automatic crossfades off. Typical values are 10-40ms.

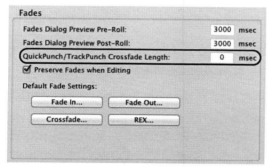

The Fades section of the Editing Preferences page

Using TrackPunch

TrackPunch mode is a variant of QuickPunch that allows you to initiate recording independently on individual tracks that have been TrackPunch-enabled. Although TrackPunch is commonly used in film and video post production workflows, it can also be useful in certain music recording situations. You could, for example, use TrackPunch to record takes with multiple musicians, punching in and out on different tracks at different points.

To start and stop recording on individual tracks using TrackPunch:

1   To enable TrackPunch, do one of the following:

    – Choose OPTIONS > TRACKPUNCH.

    – Right-click on the RECORD button and choose TrackPunch.

2   CONTROL-CLICK (Mac) or START-CLICK (Windows) on the Record Enable button for each track that you want to TrackPunch-enable. The track Record Enable buttons will light solid blue.

 An additional free voice must be held in reserve for each TrackPunch-enabled channel when using TrackPunch.

3   Click the RECORD button to arm the Transport for recording. The Record button will flash blue and red.

4   Begin playback.

5   When you want to punch in, initiate recording on any TrackPunch-enabled track by clicking on the track Record Enable button. The Track Record Enable button will light solid red during recording. You can initiate recording on any TrackPunch-enabled track at anytime during the record pass.

 OPTION-CLICK *(Mac) or* ALT-CLICK *(Windows) to initiate recording on all Track-Punch-enabled tracks. To initiate recording on selected tracks only, select two or more TrackPunch-enabled tracks and* OPTION+SHIFT-CLICK *(Mac) or* ALT+SHIFT-CLICK *(Windows) on the Record Enable button for one of the selected tracks.*

6   When you want to punch out, click the track Record Enable button on any recording track. Pro Tools will continue playing back, with recording suspended for that track (blue/red flashing Record Enable button).

7   To perform additional punch-ins, click any TrackPunch-enabled track's Record Enable button at subsequent punch-in and punch-out points.

8   When finished, stop playback and disable recording on your tracks, as needed.

Notes about QuickPunch/TrackPunch

At this point, you might be wondering why QuickPunch or TrackPunch is not enabled all the time. The reason is that some of the highly advantageous features of these recording modes may be disadvantageous when not punching in during playback.

Advantages of using QuickPunch/TrackPunch:

- You can activate instantaneous recording on-the-fly during playback.

- You can record discontiguous clips without stopping playback.

- You capture all incoming material during a playback and recording pass.
  (When you playback with QuickPunch or TrackPunch mode active, Pro Tools actually records all enabled tracks in the background, even when not punched in. This means that there is no delay when punching in, fades can extend before the punch point, and it's impossible to miss something being played by punching in too late. You can always trim the punch point as far back as needed.)

Potential Disadvantages when using QuickPunch/TrackPunch:

- Tracks that are enabled for QuickPunch recording will use twice as many voices as they would normally use, since these tracks are essentially recording and playing back audio simultaneously. This means that mono audio tracks will use two voices, stereo audio tracks will use four voices, and so on. When you are working on a very large session, you may need to deactivate some tracks to use QuickPunch or TrackPunch.

- If a number of tracks are record-enabled or TrackPunch-enabled, you may encounter a slight pause when you start playback (because Pro Tools is initiating recording in the background).

- Playback looping is not available when QuickPunch/TrackPunch is enabled with record-enabled tracks.

Recording & Compositing Multiple Takes

One of the great advantages of non-linear digital recording is that you can keep everything that you record. This has led to the widespread technique of recording multiple takes of a performance, then compositing or "comp'ing" a "best performance" by editing together the best parts from each take.

Traditionally, there have been a number of different ways to approach this technique in Pro Tools, such as recording each take to a new track, recording takes to new Playlists, and using Pro Tools' Matching Takes feature. However, Pro Tools 8 introduced functionality designed specifically for this task, resulting in a new unified workflow using Playlists.

Playlists

The contents and arrangement of audio or MIDI within a track in Pro Tools is called a Playlist. Audio and MIDI/Instrument Tracks start with a single Playlist where you record, import, and edit clips. In Module 7, you will look at Playlists in detail, and use them to experiment with different arrangements and edits within a track. Here, we discuss using Playlists as places to store, audition, and edit multiple record takes.

Playlist Basics

Every Audio, MIDI, and Instrument Track has a pop-up menu that appears to the right of its name in the Edit window (except when set to Mini or Micro height, in which case it appears in sub-menu to the left of the track name). You access this menu via the Playlist Selector, and it allows you to manage and view Edit Playlists within each track.

The Playlist Pop-up menu

The top half of the menu is used to create or duplicate Playlists in the track. The bottom half is a list of additional Playlists that you can choose for the track.

Playlist View

Pro Tools 8 added a new Playlist track view, which is accessed with the track's View Selector menu. When Playlist View is selected, Playlists associated with the track are shown as additional lanes below the Main Playlist. Additionally, this view includes a narrow, empty Playlist lane below the other Playlists. Clips can be dragged to this lane to automatically create a new Playlist.

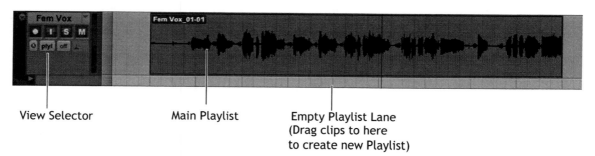

View Selector   Main Playlist   Empty Playlist Lane
                                                  (Drag clips to here
                                                  to create new Playlist)

Playlist view on a track with no alternate playlists

In the screenshot below, the Fem Vox 01 clip has been dragged from the Main Playlist to the empty Playlist lane, resulting in the creation of a new Playlist.

New Playlist created by dragging to the empty Playlist lane

Recording to Multiple Playlists

The first stage of the compositing workflow is to record multiple takes using Playlists. You can record using any of the normal record modes, and manually manage the playlists, or you can use Loop Record and have Pro Tools automatically generate new Playlists for each pass.

Recording One Take at a Time

Although Loop Recording has some advantage in this workflow (as you'll see in the next section), it's not appropriate to all recording situations or artists. In some cases, you will want to record multiple takes one at a time and manually create playlists as needed.

To record one take at a time using Playlists:

1   Record-arm the track you wish to record to.

2   Select PLAYLIST view on the track.

3   Record a take using any of the standard record modes.

4   Drag and drop the newly recorded clip(s) to the empty Playlist lane underneath the Main Playlist (as in the screenshot on the previous page). A new playlist will be generated containing the first take, and the Main Playlist will now be clear again.

 To move the clip to a new playlist without the risk of changing the timing of the clip, select the clip, and hold Control *(Mac) or* Start *(Windows) while dragging. Alternatively, select the clip and choose Clip > Time Lock/Unlock (*Shift+T*) to constrain all movement of the clip to the vertical axis.*

5   When everyone's ready, record another take into the Main Playlist.

6   Repeat steps 4 & 5 until you have enough takes.

Loop Recording

A new feature introduced in Pro Tools 8 is the ability to automatically place each pass of a Loop Record onto a new Playlist in the record track.

To record multiple takes into Playlists with Loop Record mode:

1   Enter Loop Record mode.

2   In the Operation tab of the Preferences window, check the option Automatically Create New Playlists When Loop Recording.

3   Record-arm the track you wish to record to.

4   Make a timeline selection across the range you wish to record.

5   Start Recording, and record as many takes as necessary.

6   Stop the Transport.

 The point where you press Stop is important during loop recording. If you stop less than halfway through a take, the clip for that take is discarded, and the previous take's clip will appear in the track. If you stop past half-way, the partial take's clip will appear.

When you've finished recording using either method, you'll have something that looks like the following screenshot. Note that the last take always appears in the Main Playlist.

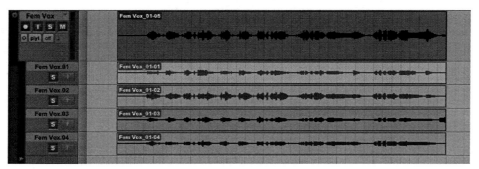

Multiple Takes on Playlists

Compositing Workflow

The next stage of the process it to put together a final performance from the takes you recorded. From a creative standpoint, many factors can influence the decisions made at this point, such as the technical quality, artistry, and continuity of the performances. From an operational point of view, Pro Tools makes it very easy to perform this process.

The following suggested workflow will guide you through the steps for comping.

1. Clear the Main Playlist

Whether you used Loop Record or recorded takes one at a time, your last take will end up on the Main Playlist. As you will be building your composite in the Main Playlist, you need to clear it. Simply drag the recording from the Main Playlist to the empty Playlist lane underneath the other Playlists, and it will be added as a new Playlist.

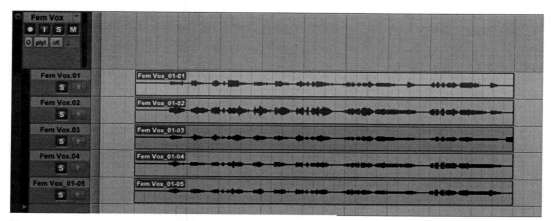

Clear the Main Playlist by moving the last take to a new playlist

2. Audition Takes

By default, only the Main Playlist plays back and can be heard. However, each of the other Playlists has a Solo button, which temporarily makes it the audible playlist.

3. Select the Best First Part

When you've decided which take you'd like to use at the start of the composite, use the Selector tool to make an Edit selection across the range you wish to use. Then press the Playlist's Copy Selection to Main Playlist button (up arrow button to the right of the Solo button).

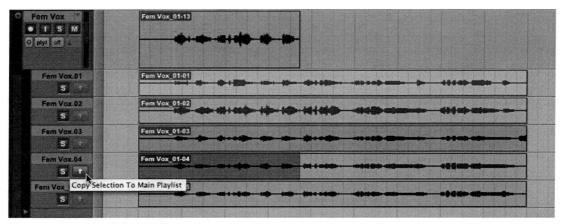

Copy first part to Main Playlist

4. Continue Copying Sections to the Main Playlist

Work your way through the performance, repeating the above procedure until you've built up a complete composite.

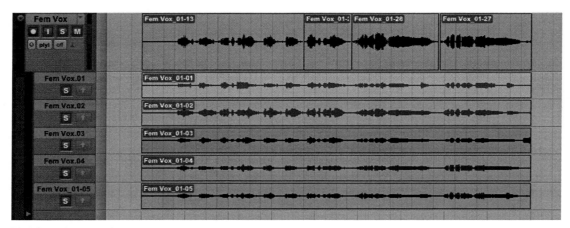

Finished Composite

5. Clean up the Main Playlist

Using Slip mode when marking sections for your composite allows you to make precise selections of the material you want, with appropriate quiet points at the cuts. However, you are likely to be left with some small gaps or other rough edits in your composite performance. In Module 5, "Professional Editing Techniques," you will learn how to tidy up a composite by trimming and using custom crossfades.

Rating Clips

One of the challenges you may face when recording and compositing multiple takes is keeping track of which takes (or partial takes) you might want to use. Pro Tools has a feature designed to help in this respect. Clips can be given a rating from 1 to 5, either during recording or when auditioning takes later.

Clip Ratings

Rating Clips at any Time During Playback

To rate a whole take do one of the following:

- Right-click on the take and choose RATING > [1-5].

- Hold down all three main modifiers, CONTROL+OPTION+COMMAND (Mac) or CTRL+START+ALT (Windows), and type the rating on the numeric keypad.

  The rating will be applied to the clip; any subsequent clips separated from this take will keep the rating.

To rate only a specific part of a take:

1   Select the section you want to rate and separate it to a new clip with the B key (in Commands Focus mode) or COMMAND+E (Mac) or CTRL+E (Windows).

2   Right-click on the new clip and choose RATING > [1-5].

View Clip Ratings in the Edit Window

To display ratings on clips in the Edit Window

- Choose VIEW > CLIP > RATING.

Filtering the Playlist View by Ratings

Once you've rated clips during recording and/or auditioning, you can choose to hide Playlists that don't contain any clips above a certain standard. This can be help the process of elimination when choosing and constructing the final composite performance.

To filter the Playlist View by Rating:

- Right-click the track name and choose Filter Lanes > Show Only Lanes With > Clips Rated >= 1-5. The view will be filtered to display only playlists containing clips rated at the chosen value or above.

- For example, selecting a value of 3 will display playlists containing clips rated 3, 4, or 5 only. This is a commonly used technique where 5 is the highest rating.

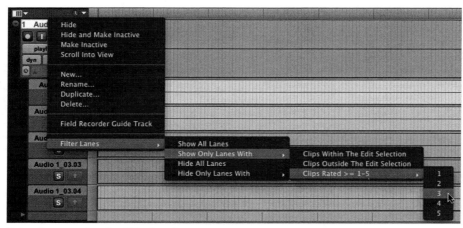

Selecting a value for filtering lanes

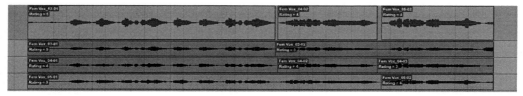

Result of filtering lanes

- Alternately, if 1 is the highest rating, you can choose to hide lanes with a certain rating or higher. If in the previous example, the highest rating was 1, choose FILTER LANES > Hide ONLY LANES WITH > CLIPS RATED >= 1-5. Selecting a value of 3 will display playlists containing clips rated 1 or 2.

Review Questions

1   Can you reposition the Dynamic Transport Play Start Marker during playback? (See "About the Play Start Marker" on page 33.)

2   What effect does Dynamic Transport mode have on the LINK TIMELINE AND EDIT SELECTION setting? (See "Moving the Timeline Selection" on page 34.)

3   Describe three ways of enabling Dynamic Transport. (See "Working in Dynamic Transport Mode" on page 32.)

4   Which input mode lets you monitor live input on tracks that are not record-enabled? (See "Monitor Modes and TrackInput" on page 37.)

5   How many running punches does QuickPunch mode allow per record take? (See "Using QuickPunch" on page 40.)

6   What are some advantages of using QuickPunch mode for recording? What are the potential disadvantages? (See "Notes about QuickPunch/TrackPunch" on page 43.)

7   What is the primary difference between QuickPunch mode and TrackPunch mode? (See "Using TrackPunch" on page 42.)

8   How can you display Playlists in lanes in the Edit window? (See "Playlist View" on page 45.)

9   When recording to automatically created playlists, where does the last take reside? (See "Loop Recording" on page 46.)

10   What are the different ways to rate a clip? (See "Rating Clips" on page 49.)

Exercise 2 Compositing From Multiple Takes

Objectives:
- Use the Playlists view for managing multiple vocal takes
- Audition takes from different playlists
- Use Clip Rating to identify preferred takes or sections for comping
- Create a composite performance from multiple recordings

Approximate Completion Time: 40 minutes.

Scenario

Your job in this exercise is to create a composite performance of a section of vocals, from a number of different takes. The vocal you will be working on is in the third verse of the 210M exercise session. Two complete lead vocal takes were recorded for the whole song, both of which are audible in the session. However, the producer decided to capture several background vocal takes for the third verse in order to add some depth.

Your task is to audition the background vocal takes, add ratings, then create a composite. There is no 'correct' result: use your own personal taste to edit the performance.

Getting Started

Open the session:

1 The session for this exercise can be found in the 210M PT10 EXERCISE 2 folder, in the location specified by your instructor (such as Audio Drive: 210M PT10 Class Files: 210M PT10 Exercise 2: 210M Exercise 2.ptx).

2 If the Missing Files dialog box opens, choose Manually Find and Relink; the files are located in the 210M PT10 EXERCISE MASTER folder in the location specified by your instructor (such as Audio Drive: 210M PT10 Class Files: 210M PT10 Exercise Master).

3 Save the session to the location specified by your instructor, with the name <your initials>210M Exercise 2.ptx.

Take a few moments to familiarize yourself with the session. The vocal track which you'll be editing is called BG Vox, and has 4 playlists. The main playlist contains the fifth take.

The section you will be editing starts at bar 52, and is indicated by a Marker named VERSE 3.

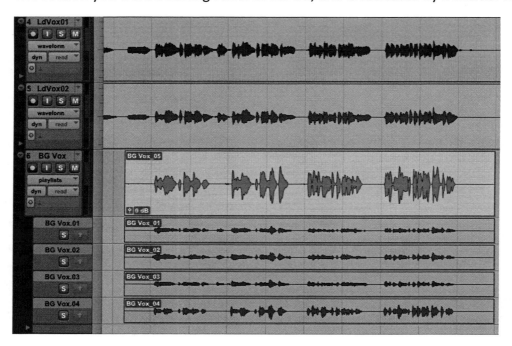

Audition and Rate the Takes [Challenge]

Task	Direction	Steps Used to Achieve Task
1	Listen to the takes by soloing each playlist in turn. Add Clip Ratings to help keep track of the sections you might want to use. Separate the takes into smaller clips if you wish to assign different ratings to sections of the same take.	

Create a composite performance [Challenge]

Task	Direction	Steps Used to Achieve Task
1	Follow the workflow in Module 2 to comp the backing vocals in the third verse. Start by clearing the main playlist, You can do this by moving the clip from the main playlist to a new playlist:	

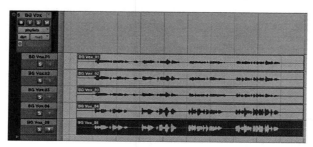

Task	Direction	Steps Used to Achieve Task
2	Copy the parts you wish to use from each take into the Main playlist.	

[Optional] Comp the rest of the vocal

If time permits, once you've finished comping the BG Vox track for the third verse, duplicate the track and comp a second background vocal track.

Task	Direction	Steps Used to Achieve Task
1	Comp a second background vocal track.	

Group Discussion

At the end of the exercise, listen to each others' results, and discuss what problems you encountered and any tricks you've learned during the tasks.

Module 3 Virtual Instruments

In this module, you will learn how to control and automate software instruments using hardware MIDI controllers. You will also study the advanced features of the Structure and Strike instruments and learn how to integrate them with the mixer using multi-channel routing schemes.

Objectives:
- Control Plug-ins with MIDI Controllers

- Record and edit MIDI Continuous Controller graphs

- Understand the difference between CC graphs and Pro Tools Automation

- Use advanced features of Structure and Strike

- Route multiple outputs from Structure and Strike to Pro Tools mixer channels

Introduction

Virtual instruments play a central role in modern computer-based music production, and you've encountered them at several times throughout the Pro Tools courses. In this module, you will investigate how to control and automate instrument plug-ins with MIDI Continuous Controllers (CCs). You will then examine two of Pro Tools' key instruments—the Structure sampler plug-in and Strike virtual drummer plug-in—and explore some of their deeper features and uses. Finally, you will learn how you can route multiple audio channels from these plug-ins, allowing you to manage several sources from a single plug-in instance across multiple tracks in the main Pro Tools mixer.

Using Virtual Instruments with Control Surfaces and MIDI Controllers

Avid Control Surfaces

Virtual instrument parameters can be controlled from any Avid control surface. This is achieved in the same way as controlling any other Pro Tools plug-in from the surface. Avid control surfaces are integrated into the automation system of Pro Tools and can automatically take control of any parameter that appears in the automation list.

 By default, the order in which parameters appear on the surface is pre-determined. However, Pro Tools includes plug-in mapping functionality that allows you to re-map plug-in parameters to any available control on an Avid control surface. See the Pro Tools 205 and Pro Tools 310I courses to learn how to map plug-ins to controls on each control surface.

MIDI Controllers

Many MIDI keyboards and control surfaces have assignable knobs and sliders that are ideal for controlling virtual instruments. Unlike with Avid control surfaces, this support is not built into Pro Tools' plug-in functionality. Instead, this is achieved using standard MIDI CC (Continuous Controller) messages. CC events are MIDI messages that allow you to control the parameters of a MIDI device in real time.

Assigning MIDI Controls to Plug-in Parameters

Instrument plug-ins tend to support MIDI control in one of the following two ways:

- Fixed CC assignments—Parameters are programmed to respond to particular CC messages. If this is the case, you will need to configure controls on your MIDI keyboard or surface to transmit using the correct controller number.

- Editable/Learnable CC assignments—Parameters can be assigned to any CC code. This removes the need to edit your hardware controller or keyboard. Often, plug-ins feature a "learn" mode, allowing you to tell a parameter to pick up and follow the next incoming MIDI controller message.

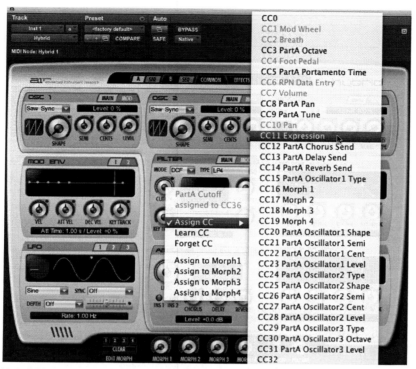

Hybrid has pre-assigned CC mappings, and can also learn new ones.

The image above shows Hybrid's support for MIDI CC control. Right-clicking on a control (in this case the Filter Cutoff knob) brings up options to Assign the control to a specific CC.

Recording MIDI CC Data

Plug-ins that support the "Learn CC" feature provide a quick and easy way for a MIDI controller's knob, fader, etc., to be mapped to the desired parameter in the plug-in.

To use the "Learn CC" feature:

1 Right-click the plug-in control that you wish to assign to a MIDI controller's control.

2 Choose "Learn CC from the menu that appears.

3 On the MIDI controller, move the controller that you wish to assign to the plug-in parameter. The plug-in will respond to the motion of the hardware control, indicating that the CC has been correctly assigned to the plug-in parameter.

CC values and moves can be recorded into MIDI and Instrument Tracks. The CC data is recorded in the same way as MIDI notes (i.e., by record-arming the track and performing a record pass), and the CC data is written into the same MIDI clips as notes (unlike Pro Tools automation, which is separate from MIDI or audio clips). As a result, different Edit playlists on a MIDI or Instrument track can have different CC event graphs.

 Make sure that MIDI Merge mode is active whenever you're recording CC data over an existing performance. Otherwise, the existing MIDI data on the track will be overwritten.

Viewing and Editing Recorded MIDI CC Data

Pro Tools displays CC data as graphs in the Edit window, much like automation.

To display and edit Continuous Controller data:

1   In the Edit window, click the track's Track View selector and choose the CC data type you wish to view or edit (either from the top portion of the menu or from the CONTROLLERS submenu). The corresponding CC event graph will display in the track.

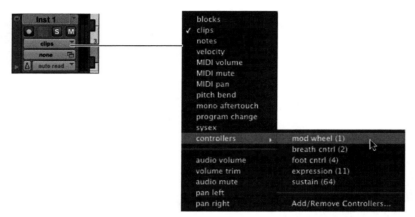

— If you've not yet recorded anything for the CC type you wish to view, it may not appear in the list for viewing. In this case, choose CONTROLLERS > ADD/REMOVE CONTROLLER. The AUTOMATED MIDI CONTROLLERS dialog box will open, allowing you to select the continuous controllers that you wish to display/edit. Select the track you wish to modify (or ALL TRACKS), the desired controller type(s), click ADD, then click OK.

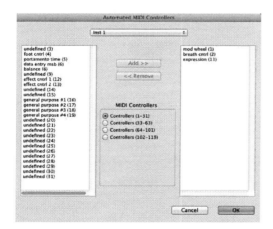

2   You can edit a CC event graph in any of the following ways:

— Draw with the Pencil, either freehand or using any of the shapes and line/curve drawing tools.

— Drag breakpoints with the Grabber tool to adjust their locations or values.

— Scale a group of selected breakpoints up or down with the Trim tool.

— Rearrange controller events using standard edit operations, such as Copy, Paste, Nudge, and Shift.

Automation vs. MIDI CC Graphs

MIDI and Instrument Tracks are able to record both 'regular' Pro Tools automation and MIDI CC data. Both appear as graphs in their own track playlists, and both can be used for similar purposes, but they are fundamentally different:

- CC data is recorded in the same way as MIDI notes or audio, rather than with dedicated automation writing modes.

- CC data cannot be recorded by moving a virtual instrument parameter with the mouse during a record pass; it can only be recorded from a MIDI controller device.

- CC data is written into MIDI clips, and each Edit playlist has its own CC event graphs for each parameter; by contrast, only one Pro Tools automation playlist exists for each automatable parameter on a track.

- CC event graphs are static between breakpoints, creating a stepped graph as values change. Pro Tools automation playlists are vector-based, so parameters move smoothly between breakpoints.

- CC data has lower resolution and timing accuracy than Pro Tools automation.

- CC event graphs are not continuous in the same sense as automation. In other words, parameters are not locked to the graph at all times, only where data exists. So you can move the parameter freely outside of areas that have been recorded. This can cause inconsistencies with playback from one pass to the next.

When to Record MIDI or Automation

Recording MIDI CC moves is often best when you need to record a MIDI take that includes controller moves as part of the performance (for example when using the Mod Wheel to modulate the sound while playing notes in one record pass).

In other circumstances, such as when modulating a synth's parameters as a separate pass from note recording, Pro Tools' native plug-in automation is often the better choice. This is due to its superior resolution, interpolation, and the fact that parameters are locked to the graph throughout a song. It's important to note that you can still use your MIDI device to control the parameter as you record the automation. The difference is that you are writing automation generated by the parameter movements, rather than recording MIDI from the hardware controller.

Routing Multiple Outputs from Plug-ins

By default, a plug-in's audio output routes to the mixer channel on which the plug-in is inserted. However, Pro Tools' plug-in and mixer architecture allows some plug-ins to make their audio outputs available to any channel in the mixer. This allows you to split out sounds from multi-timbral instruments, drum kits, etc., and route them to mixer channels on the Pro Tools mixer as an alternative to using the plug-in's own internal mixer structure.

Some examples of plug-ins that support multiple output routing include the following:

- Structure – Patches, Parts, and Global Sends can all be independently routed out of the plug-in.

- Strike – Individual channels from the Mix page (including the Overheads, Room, and Talkback channels) can be routed to separate outputs.

- Transfuser – Individual Tracks and the two global effects returns can be routed to separate outputs.

In this section we'll look at two examples, using the Structure and Strike plug-ins.

Using Structure as a Multi-Timbral Sound Source

The Structure plug-in allows you to load multiple Patches, each with its own MIDI channel. Structure also has 32 stereo output assignments that can be used to bus signals to other tracks in the Pro Tools mixer. This makes it possible to use a single instance of Structure for many different sound sources within a session. As well as being more flexible and efficient than using multiple instances of Structure, this means you can easily save and re-use the multi-timbral presets you create in Structure.

Structure can have independent outputs at both the Patch and Part level. This gives you a high degree of flexibility in setting up your routing. You can, for example, have a Patch that responds to a particular MIDI channel, but with internal Parts that route to separate outputs.

Structure Example: Setting up a Multi-Timbral String Bank

In this example, we'll set up a powerful orchestral string sound source, comprising four Patches in Structure: Bass, Cello, Viola, and Violin. Each of these sample patches will be played and monitored via an individual Instrument Track.

1. Create an Aux Input Track and insert Structure

Often Structure is inserted on an Instrument Track, but in this example, all the MIDI inputs to the plug-in will be coming from other tracks, so an Aux Input will suffice.

2. Add Patches to Structure

This example uses four patches from the EWQL Orchestral Elements folder of the factory patch library: Contrabass Section Legato, Cello Section Legato, Viola Section Legato, and Violin Section Legato. Use the PATCH > ADD PATCH command from Structure's menus to add these patches.

3. Set Patches to Different Outputs

Each Patch has its own Audio Out in the main Patch List, which is also repeated in the Output tab. Set each of these to a different output, starting with Out 2. (Out 1 is Structure's master output and routes to the track where the plug-in is inserted.)

4. Set the Patches to Different MIDI Channels

By default, each Patch you add is assigned to a discrete MIDI channel, so this step is completed automatically.

Patch
Audio
Output
Selector

Patch
MIDI
Channel
Selector

Global
Send
Output
Selector

Structure Multi Patch

5. [Optional] Set Global Send Outputs

Each Patch has four sends to Structure's Global Send buses. These buses can be routed to any of Structure's 32 outputs. This allows you to bring up send effects on an Aux Input track in Pro Tools for easy control. You can also leave the Send's Inserts empty, which provides a clean send from Structure which you can then process with other Pro Tools plug-ins. Alternatively, you can simply use the Sends on the Pro Tools channels and not use Structure's Sends at all. In our example, the Patches all share a reverb on Send 1, which is then routed to a channel in Pro Tools via Out 6.

6. Create Instrument Tracks and Route MIDI

For each Patch in Structure, create a stereo Instrument Track, and set its MIDI output to the corresponding channel in Structure.

7. Set Audio Inputs to Structure Channels

On each of the Instrument Tracks, click the audio input selector, and choose the relevant Structure channel from the plug-in sub-menu.

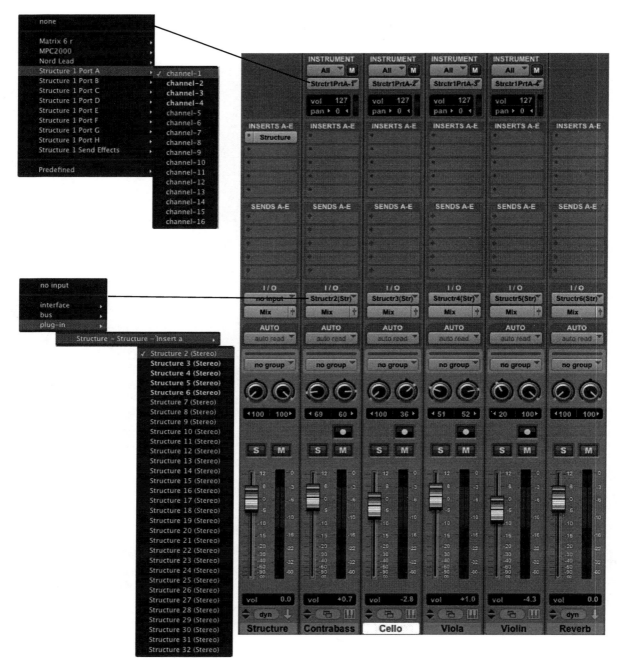

Routing Multiple Sound Sources from Structure.

Mixing Strike Drums on the Main Mixer

Although Strike has a comprehensive internal mixer with onboard effects, it is sometimes advantageous to split channels out from the plug-in to the main mixer. This allows processing with other plug-ins, and brings up the channels on Pro Tools' main mixer, facilitating easy automation with a control surface. In many situations you will only need to separate one or two channels, but in the following example, we split out an entire Strike kit to emulate a multi-mic'ed drum recording on the Pro Tools mixer.

1. Create an Instrument Track

Unlike the Structure example, we'll be controlling Strike from a single MIDI source, so this time we'll use an Instrument Track for the plug-in.

2. Route Channels in the Mix Page

Once a Style and Kit have been loaded, the individual channels can be routed in the Mix Page. Each of the 8 available outputs is stereo. To save outputs, you can route two mono channels to the same output and pan them left and right (as with the Kick and Snare in the screen below). Instrument channels may also be submixed by sharing an output (for example blending all the Toms within Strike, and assigning their outputs to stereo Output 4).

As well as the individual instrument channels, you can route the additional mic sources (Overheads, Room, and Talkback). Anything that remains routed to the Master will be routed through the Instrument Track on which Strike is inserted. In the example, the Talkback mic is the only channel left routed to the Master.

3. Create Tracks in the Mixer and Route Inputs

Each of the individual sources you've routed requires a mono or stereo track to bring that bus into the main mixer. This time, we'll use Audio Tracks set to Input Monitoring mode, as described in Module 2. Aux Input Tracks can also be used, but using Audio Tracks saves times if you need to record the individual outputs. In the Exercise following this module, you will set up and record multiple outputs from a plug-in.

4. Other Options

Several other settings have been made in this example, and are described in the next picture. These settings will vary depending on the situation. In this example we are using the Pro Tools mixer for all the mixing tasks, but at other times a mixture of Pro Tools' and Strike internal mixers and effects may be preferred.

Channel
Output
Selector

Effects are off in this example as all
processing is being performed in the
main Pro Tools mixer

Room and Overhead sends have
all been zeroed.

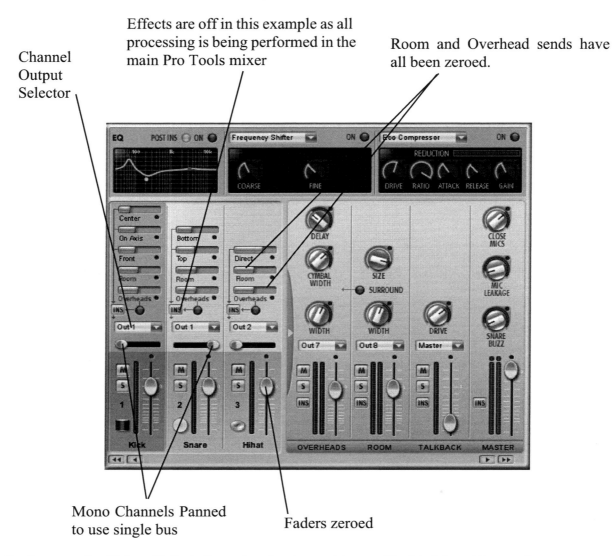

Mono Channels Panned
to use single bus

Faders zeroed

Routing an entire kit from Strike to the main mixer to emulate a multi-mic'ed drum kit recording

Strike assigned to an Instrument Track
as only one MIDI input needed

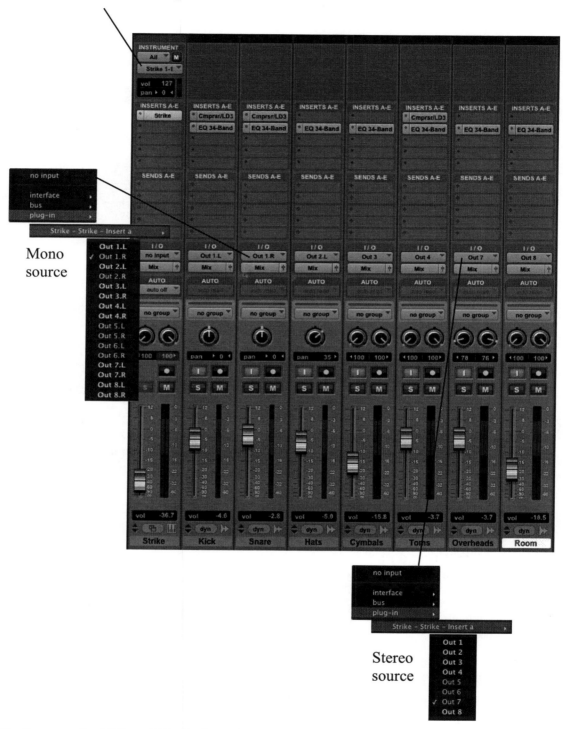

Mono
source

Stereo
source

Routing an entire kit from Strike to the main mixer

Review Questions

1   What are some differences between an automation playlist and a continuous controller event graph? (See "Automation vs. MIDI CC Graphs" on page 63.)

2   How would you record automated changes to an existing MIDI performance using CC data? How is the CC data affected by the track's Automation mode? (See "Recording MIDI CC Data" on page 61.)

3   What are some examples of multi-timbral plug-ins that support multiple output routing? (See "Routing Multiple Outputs from Plug-ins" on page 64.)

4   How many stereo outputs does Structure have for bussing signals to other tracks in the Pro Tools mixer? (See "Using Structure as a Multi-Timbral Sound Source" on page 64.)

5   How many stereo outputs does Strike have? How can you maximize the number of outputs available for individual drum channels? (See "Mixing Strike Drums on the Main Mixer" on page 67.)

6   When routing a specific output from a plug-in such as Structure to another track, where would you assign the input for the destination track (using what selector)? (See "Using Structure as a Multi-Timbral Sound Source" on page 64.)

7   Why might you want to route multiple outputs from an instrument plug-in to different tracks? (See "Routing Multiple Outputs from Plug-ins" on page 64.)

Exercise 3   Plug-in Routing

Objectives:

- Route several different parts from a Structure plug-in to separate tracks in the mixer.

- Set up a mix of the new elements.

Approximate Completion Time: 25 minutes.

Introduction

This exercise is an opportunity to use Pro Tools' internal plug-in routing functionality. This 210M Session has an Instrument track called Structure hosting an instance of the Structure plug-in. Bass, Cello, Viola, and Violin parts have been loaded into Structure. Your task in this exercise is to route the parts out to separate tracks, apply individual effects, and prepare to record the tracks as audio.

Getting Started

Open the session:

1   The session for this exercise will be in the 210M P10 Exercise 3 folder, in the location specified by your instructor (such as Audio Drive: 210M PT10 Class Files: 210M PT10 Exercise 3: 210M Exercise 3.ptx)

2   If the Missing Files dialog box opens, choose Manually Find and Relink; the files are located in the 210M PT10 Exercise Master folder in the location specified by your instructor (such as Audio Drive: 210M PT10 Class Files: 210M PT10 Exercise Master).

3   Save the session to the location specified by your instructor, with the name <your initials>210M Exercise 3.ptx.

Open the Plug-in and Audition it from a Keyboard

1   Find the track Structure, and click on the Structure plug-in to open its window. There are four parts within the Structure preset.

2   Select the Structure track so your MIDI keyboard will send notes to Structure.

3   Play the parts from your MIDI keyboard.

Route the First Part to a Separate Mixer Track [Guided]

1   Create a stereo audio track next to the Structure track, and name it Basses.

2   Click the Input Selector on the new track, choose Plug-in, and then choose "Structure 2 (Stereo)."

3   In Structure, set the Audio Out of the Basses part to Out 2 (remember that Out 1 is reserved for the Structure plug-in's own playout).

4   Switch the new audio track to Input Monitor mode.

5   Play the part on your MIDI keyboard. The audio from the Basses part should now be appearing at the new audio track instead of the Structure track.

Route the Other Parts [Challenge]

Task	Direction	Steps Used to Achieve Task
1	Route the other three parts to new stereo audio tracks (in this case, use Audio tracks rather than Aux Inputs so you can easily record the signals later).	

Set Up Levels and Effects on the Parts [Challenge]

Task	Direction	Steps Used to Achieve Task
1	Using the new tracks, set fader levels and pan settings appropriate to the mix. The original Structure track had a Reverb send that was being used to process the combined output of the plug-in. Try to recreate this on each audio track.	

Next Steps

In Exercise 4, you will return to this session and create a MIDI sequence that plays the parts in the song. You will then record the finished tracks as audio.

Module 4 Advanced MIDI Production

This module looks at a variety of advanced techniques for working with MIDI Data. We explore techniques for improving your MIDI recordings, advanced methods of MIDI editing, and real-time processing options, as well as other powerful ways of improving your workflow when working in a MIDI environment.

Objectives:

- Use the MIDI Editor window

- Use the Groove Quantize operations

- Use the Flatten and Restore Performance operations

- Use the Change Velocity operations

- Use advanced features of MIDI Real-Time Properties

- Understand the basic features of the Score Editor window

The MIDI Editor Window

Although it's possible to perform MIDI editing tasks directly on MIDI and Instrument Tracks within the Edit window, Pro Tools also offers a dedicated MIDI Editor window. The MIDI Editor window offers a number of powerful advantages:

- You can easily make fine adjustments to notes, velocities, and automation in the MIDI Editor window while working on the overall arrangement in the Edit window.

- You can maintain separate settings and modes for the MIDI Editor and Edit windows. For example, you can have different Edit Modes, Edit Tools, Zoom settings, Scroll Mode, Nudge and Grid values, etc. in each window. This allows you to switch between modes/tools appropriate to arrangement and fine editing tasks very quickly, or between editing Audio and MIDI parts.

- Notes, velocities, controller data, and automation are displayed on separate lanes in the MIDI Editor, allowing you to see any desired parameters simultaneously.

- You can display and edit notes and velocity data from multiple MIDI/Instrument Tracks in a unified piano roll environment. Data from different tracks can be differentiated by color-coding.

- You can also view MIDI as musical notation in the timeline and switch quickly between traditional notation and a piano roll view.

Viewing MIDI Editor Windows

You can open multiple MIDI Editor windows, each of which can provide a unique view of MIDI in your Pro Tools session. Like Plug-in, Output, and Send windows, a single MIDI Editor window can be "targeted." A MIDI Editor can also be shown "docked" at the bottom of the Edit window.

To open a MIDI Editor Window:

- Choose WINDOW > MIDI EDITOR or type CONTROL+= (Mac) or START+= (Windows).

- A MIDI Editor Window will open at the current timeline selection.

If no MIDI or Instrument tracks are selected, the top-most MIDI or Instrument track will be shown when the MIDI Editor is opened. Often, a more useful option is to select the tracks that you wish to view in the MIDI Editor window before you open it (the selected tracks will be shown).

The MIDI Editor Window

Opening a MIDI Editor window from the Window menu opens the MIDI Editor in a separate, stand-alone window:

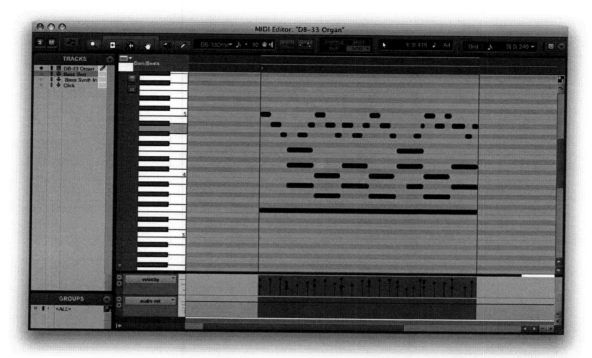

MIDI Editor Window

To open a MIDI Editor window to display a specific selection:

1   Make an Edit Selection in the Edit window.

2   Choose WINDOW > MIDI EDITOR.

    – A MIDI Editor window will open that is centered on the current Edit Selection, and Pro Tools will display all tracks covered by the selection.

You can also open the MIDI Editor to display a specific MIDI clip.

To open a MIDI Editor window for a specific clip:

1   In the MIDI tab of the Preferences make sure that the option DOUBLE-CLICKING A MIDI CLIP OPENS THE: is set to MIDI EDITOR.

2   Select the Grabber Tool.

3   Do one of the following:

    – Double-click a MIDI clip.

    – Right-click in the open MIDI Editor window and select OPEN IN NEW MIDI EDITOR.

To open additional MIDI Editor windows do one of the following:

- Deselect the Target button in the open MIDI Editor window and open another MIDI Editor window.

- Right-click in the open MIDI Editor window and select Open in Untargeted MIDI Editor.

The Docked MIDI Editor

An alternative to opening a MIDI Editor in a separate window, the docked MIDI Editor can be displayed as an element within the Edit window. In this case, the Edit window switches to a split view, with the normal Edit window display at the top, and the MIDI Editor at the bottom.

MIDI Editor Window

To view the MIDI Editor docked in the Edit Window do one of the following:

- Choose VIEW > OTHER DISPLAYS > MIDI EDITOR.

- Choose MIDI EDITOR in the Edit window's drop-down View Menu (located in the upper right-hand corner of the Edit window).

The Contents of the MIDI Editor Window

The MIDI Editor is laid out similarly to the Edit window; it has many of the same controls, some of which are linked to the Edit window and some of which are independent. The MIDI Editor window displays the timeline, and shares the same Timeline and Edit Selections as the Edit window. Changes to selections in any window are instantly reflected in the Edit window and other MIDI Editor windows.

Tracks Display

The MIDI Editor displays a single, continuous piano roll or notation display. If multiple tracks are displayed in a MIDI Editor, their MIDI notes are shown superimposed on the same piano roll and may be, color-coded by track (by clicking the "Color by Track" button, which will be discussed later in this module). In Notation view, separate tracks are shown on dedicated staves. MIDI Editors can also display controller and automation lanes below the main MIDI/notation display. This allows you to view and edit performance and automation data on MIDI, Instrument, and Aux Input tracks alongside notes.

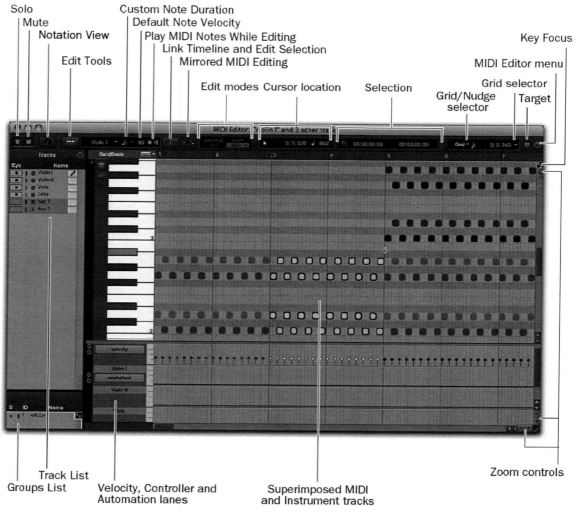

MIDI Editor window

Track List

The Track List has the same appearance in MIDI Editors as in the Edit and Mix windows, except for an additional Pencil Column in the MIDI Editor. Clicking in this column determines which track will be affected by use of the Pencil Tool (multiple tracks can be simultaneously edited with the Pencil tool using methods similar to showing and hiding multiple tracks). You can manually show and hide tracks using the Show/Hide icons (black/gray dots) in the Track List (in the Targeted MIDI Editor, tracks will be shown and hidden automatically to reflect the current Edit Selection in the Edit window).

Piano Roll View

In Piano Roll view, the main display behaves in much the same way as a MIDI or Instrument Track set to Notes view in the Edit window. However, the MIDI Editor is different in that when more than one track is displayed in a MIDI Editor, all the notes from all tracks are displayed and edited on the same Piano Roll.

Two MIDI Tracks displayed in the MIDI Editor, color coded by track

Color Coding Notes

When multiple tracks are displayed, color coding helps to indicate which notes belong to which track. Two buttons to the left of the piano roll display change the color-coding modes.

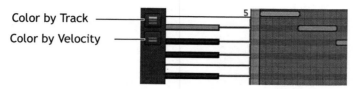

Color by Track
Color by Velocity

- Color Coding by Clip Color—This is the default color scheme, and is active when both the color code buttons are off. In this mode, MIDI notes have the same color as their clips in the Edit window.

- Color Coding by Track—Tracks in the MIDI Editor Track List are assigned various colors. These are used to color code notes in the piano roll when Color Code by Track mode is selected.

- Color Coding by Velocity—When Color Coding by Velocity is enabled, MIDI notes all have the same red hue on all displayed tracks, and MIDI notes vary in color saturation (from a light red to a dark red) based on the Note On velocity. Notes with low velocities are lighter in color, and those with high velocities are darker.

Notation View

The Notes pane in MIDI Editor windows can also display MIDI notes in standard music notation. In Notation view, each MIDI and Instrument Track is displayed independently, with one track per staff (Grand Staff, Treble, Bass, Alto, or Tenor). In MIDI Editor windows, notation is displayed as a continuous timeline and not in page view as in the Score Editor window (discussed later in this module).

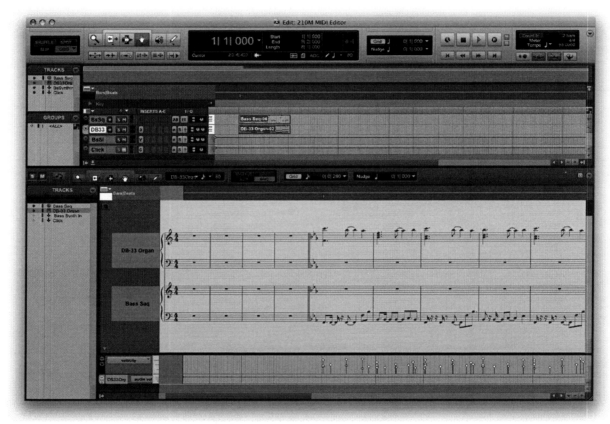

The same selection as the previous screen shown in Notation View

To enable Notation View:

- Enable the Notation View button in the MIDI Editor window.

Velocity, Controller, and Automation Lanes

MIDI Editor windows let you edit velocities, MIDI controller data, and automation for all shown MIDI, Instrument, and Auxiliary Input tracks in lanes under the Notes pane. You can move and resize Automation and Controller lanes just like in the Edit window. When viewing multiple MIDI and Instrument Tracks, the velocities for notes on separate tracks are superimposed in a single lane, just like notes in the Notes pane. However, all other Controller lanes are grouped by automation and controller type, and provide individual lanes for each shown track (lane coloring follows track colors as displayed in the Tracks list).

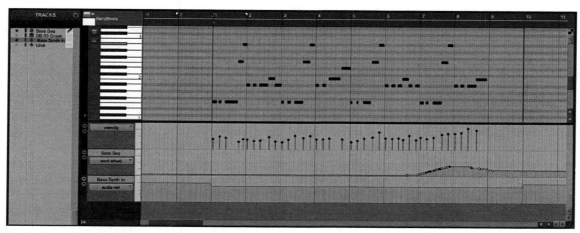

Controller / Automation Lanes

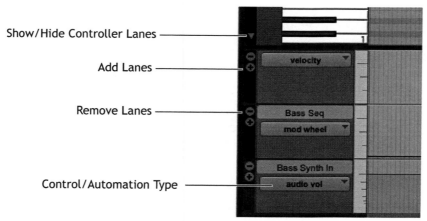

Show/Hide Controller Lanes

Add Lanes

Remove Lanes

Control/Automation Type

Controller / Automation Lane controls

MIDI Editor Window Toolbar

The MIDI Editor window toolbar is similar to the Edit window toolbar, but with a few exceptions. Each MIDI Editor window and the Edit window can be configured independently of one another. For example, you can have Notation view enabled in one MIDI Editor window, but not another; or, you can have a MIDI Editor window set to Grid mode, but the Edit window set to Slip mode. You can also customize the toolbar in each MIDI Editor window.

Solo and Mute Buttons

The Solo and Mute buttons let you solo or mute tracks currently displayed in the MIDI Editor window. These buttons duplicate the main mute and solo buttons found in the Mix and Edit windows.

Edit Modes

The Edit modes in MIDI Editor windows function exactly the same way for MIDI data as in the Edit window. Edit mode settings are unique to each MIDI Editor window and are also set independently of the Edit window.

> *When a MIDI Editor is in Notation view, only Grid mode is available.*

Edit Tools

The Edit tools in MIDI Editor windows can be displayed as a single, condensed tool with a pop-up menu for selecting other tools, or as an expanded, complete row of Edit tool icons just like in the Edit window (by clicking the "Expanded Edit Tools" item in the MIDI Editor window's drop-down View Menu located in the upper right-hand corner of the MIDI Editor window). The Edit tools in MIDI Editor windows function in the same way as in the Edit window.

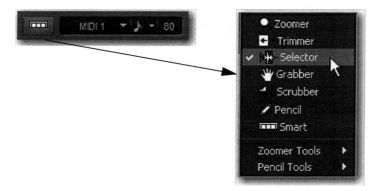

Track Edit Selector

If more than one MIDI or Instrument Track is shown in the MIDI Editor window, the Track Edit selector lets you select which track is "pencil- enabled." You can edit the automation and controller data for the pencil-enabled track in the Automation and Controller lanes under the Notes pane in the MIDI Editor window. You can also pencil-enable a track in the Track List.

Target

Generally, the Target button for MIDI Editor windows functions just like the Target button for Plug-in, Output, and Send windows. There can only be one targeted MIDI Editor window at a time. One or more un-targeted MIDI Editor windows can remain open and available at the same time, just like un-targeted Plug-in windows. Targeting an un-targeted MIDI Editor window disables any other targeted MIDI Editor window. The front-most window, regardless of whether it is targeted, always receives Keyboard Command focus and control surface focus.

Additionally, the Target button in a MIDI Editor window synchronizes the Window's Timeline location view to the Timeline location view in the Edit window. Any changes to the Edit selection in the Edit window are reflected in the targeted MIDI Editor window. The targeted MIDI Editor window can also be stored in a Window Configuration.

Target Enabled

Enhancing Performances

In this section, you will learn several functions available in the Event Operations suite that build upon ideas from previous courses.

Groove Quantize

In the Pro Tools 110 course, you learned how to use the Quantize page of the Event Operations window to apply Grid Quantization to align notes/events to a specified timing grid. You can also use the dialog box to apply Groove Quantization.

The Groove Quantize process adjusts locations, velocities, and durations of MIDI notes, or the location of Events in an Elastic Audio clip, according to a groove template rather than a strict quantization grid. Groove templates map the rhythmic and dynamic variations, or feel, within a performance.

 Beat Detective can be used to extract the groove from MIDI and audio clips. The feel of one recorded performance can then be applied to other MIDI or Elastic Audio clips. Alternatively, you can apply grooves from the preset library.

Applying Groove Quantize

Groove templates can be any length and can be applied to any number of bars. If you choose a selection that is longer than the groove template, the template will be looped as needed.

Though it's most common to apply groove templates to passages in the same meter as the groove template, there's nothing to stop you from doing otherwise. If a groove template is applied to a track selection with a different meter, the template will be repeated or truncated to match the number of beats in the selection. The groove template will always be mapped such that the downbeats are aligned with the selection downbeats, and only the appropriate number of beats from the groove template will be applied to each measure. Thus, it is not necessary to start on the downbeat when making a selection to apply a groove template.

To apply Groove Quantize:

1 Select the section to be Groove Quantized.

2 Choose EVENT > EVENT OPERATIONS > QUANTIZE, or press OPTION+0 (Mac) or ALT+0 (Windows). The Event Operations dialog box will open with the Quantize page displayed.

3 Select a groove template from the Quantize Grid pop-up menu.

4 Select the desired settings for the Quantize Grid and other available options (see "Groove Quantize Options" below).

5 Click APPLY.

Groove Quantize Options

In the Pro Tools 110 course, you learned about the What to Quantize options in the Quantize window. You will now explore the remaining options, which allow you to customize the way in which a groove is applied to your performance.

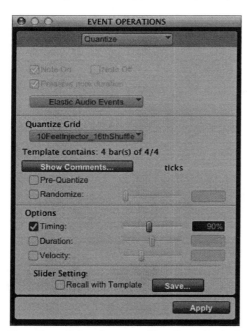

Quantize dialog box - audio clip selected

- Pre-Quantize: This option will hard quantize the timings of notes/events to a 16th-note grid before applying the groove template. If you don't use this option, your notes will be moved by the Timing percentage toward the template from their recorded positions, instead of from the grid.

- Randomize: This option moves notes/events randomly forward or backward in time after quantization occurs, to provide a more natural sounding performance. The setting of the percentage slider determines the amount of deviation allowed in the randomization.

- Timing: This option influences the timing of the selected MIDI notes or Elastic Audio events. The slider changes the amount of quantization applied to the selection.

  - 0% or deselected – No change in timing

  - 1 to 100% – Notes/events move toward the underlying template locations by the percentage amount

  - 101 to 200% – Notes/events move beyond the underlying template locations, producing an exaggerated effect on the timing; typically used with the Pre-Quantize option enabled to overemphasize the groove feel relative to the straight timing of the Grid

- Duration: This option influences the durations of the selected MIDI notes. The slider sets the amount of change applied to note durations.

  - 0% or deselected – No change in durations

  - 1 to 100% – Durations increase or decrease to more closely match the durations in the groove template; at 100% the note durations match those in the template

  - 101 to 200% – Durations increase and decrease beyond the amount required to match the template durations; the resulting durations deviate from template durations in opposite directions relative to the original performance

- Velocity: This option influences the velocities of the selected MIDI notes. The slider sets the amount of change applied to note velocities.

  - 0% or deselected – No change to velocities

  - 1 to 100% – Velocities are changed to more closely match the velocities in the current groove template; at 100% the note velocities match those in the template

  - 101 to 200% – Velocity changes are over-exaggerated, exceeding the amount required to match the template velocities; the resulting velocities deviate from template velocities in opposite directions relative to the original performance

The Slider Settings section of the dialog box provides two additional options for the Timing, Duration, and Velocity options: RECALL WITH TEMPLATE and SAVE.

- Recall with Template: This option enables you to recall the Timing, Duration, and Velocity slider settings that are saved with a groove template. Enabling this option will reset the sliders the next time you select a groove template.

- Save: This option enables you to save a groove template with the current Timing, Duration, and Velocity slider settings.

Restore Performance

The Restore Performance command allows you to remove the effects of certain Event Operations applied to MIDI notes or Elastic Audio events.

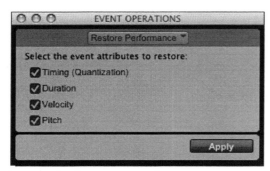

Restore Performance window

Any changes that you've made through the standard Quantize, Groove Quantize, Change Duration, Change Velocity, or Change Pitch commands, as well as pitch changes you've made in conjunction with a Key Change event, can be undone with this command, and the attributes of the original (or flattened, as you'll learn in the next section) performance will be restored.

Restore Performance does not undo cut, copied, pasted, or otherwise manually moved or edited MIDI notes. To safeguard against these operations, create a new playlist prior to editing (see Module 8), or save copies of recorded clips that you can return to.

To undo all Event Operation changes to a performance:

1   Select the MIDI or Elastic Audio to be restored.

2   Choose EVENT > EVENT OPERATIONS > RESTORE PERFORMANCE.

3   Select the attributes to restore.

4   Click APPLY.

Restore Performance can be used to roll changes back to the original performance, or to roll back to a previously defined baseline state created with the Flatten Performance command (see next section), even after a session has been saved and the Undo queue lost.

Flatten Performance

The Flatten Performance command creates a new "restore to" state for the specified note attributes (timing, duration, velocity, or pitch). When you flatten note attributes, the original performance information for those attributes is permanently replaced with the current information. The flattened attribute values become the new baseline values for the Restore Performance command.

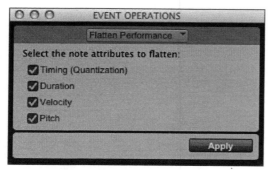

Flatten Performance window

To flatten a performance:

1 Select the MIDI or Elastic Audio clips that you wish to flatten.

2 Choose EVENT > EVENT OPERATIONS > FLATTEN PERFORMANCE.

3 Select the attributes to flatten.

4 Click APPLY.

The Change Velocity Operation

In the Pro Tools 110 course, you learned how to edit MIDI note velocities individually with the Grabber, or in groups by drawing a line across several notes with the Pencil tool. Velocities can also be manipulated using the Event Operation Change Velocity command.

The Change Velocity command can adjust attack and release velocities for selected MIDI notes. You can use this command to modify velocities in a variety of ways, including creating non-linear crescendos and decrescendos.

To adjust the velocities of a group of selected MIDI notes:

1 Select the notes that need to be adjusted.

2 Choose EVENT > EVENT OPERATIONS > CHANGE VELOCITY. The MIDI Operations dialog box will open, with the Change Velocity page displayed.

3 In the Change Velocity dialog box, enable the desired options and modify settings as needed (see "Change Velocity Options" below).

4 Click APPLY.

Change Velocity Options

The options available in the Change Velocity dialog box determine how the command will affect selected MIDI notes.

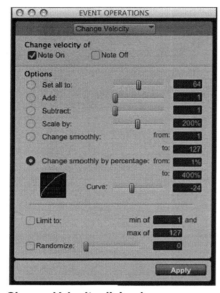

Change Velocity dialog box

- Set all to: Select this option to set all velocities to the same value, as specified by the slider.

- Add: Select this option to increase all velocities by the specified value.

- Subtract: Select this option to decrease all velocities by the specified value.

- Scale by: Select this option to scale all velocities by a percentage of their current values. Percentages below 100% scale velocities down; percentages above 100% scale velocities up.

- Change smoothly: Select this option to create a smooth velocity ramp-up (crescendo) or ramp-down (decrescendo) over time.

  – Enter starting and ending velocity values in the FROM and TO fields, respectively.

  – Adjust the CURVE slider as desired to set the shape of the ramp-up or ramp-down.

- Change smoothly by percentage: Select this option to create a smooth velocity ramp-up or ramp-down over time, based on percentages of the original values. This option enables you to preserve velocity relationships between notes while creating an overall velocity change over time.

  – Enter starting and ending percentage values in the FROM and TO fields, respectively.

  – Adjust the CURVE slider as desired to set the shape of the ramp-up or ramp-down.

- Limit to: Select this option to restrict changes made by the Change Velocity command to a specified velocity range. This setting applies to all options except SET TO ALL.

- Randomize: Select this option to apply random variations to the velocities. A randomized value (+/-) is added to the results of the Change Velocity command based on the specified percentage.

Real-Time MIDI Properties In Depth

Pro Tools 110 introduced the concept of MIDI Real-Time Properties, and described how to add grid quantize to a MIDI track in real time. We will now explore real-time MIDI processing in depth.

You can apply real-time processing to your MIDI data using either track-based Real-Time Properties, which affect an entire track or tracks, or clip-based Real-Time Properties, which affect only selected clips.

Track-Based Real-Time Properties

As you learned in the Pro Tools 110 course, MIDI and Instrument Tracks have a Real-Time Properties Edit window view, accessed from the Edit Window View selector or by choosing VIEW > EDIT WINDOW > REAL-TIME PROPERTIES. You can also set the Real-Time properties of a track from the floating Real-Time Properties window, by selecting the appropriate track in the APPLY TO pop-up (see next section).

Any settings made in the Real-Time Properties column view are track-based and will normally affect all MIDI clips in the track, including any clip that is subsequently dropped onto the track. However, clips with existing clip-based properties will ignore track-based settings.

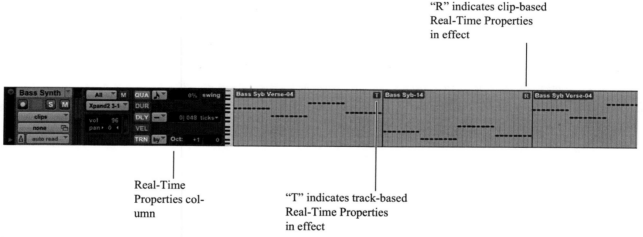

"R" indicates clip-based Real-Time Properties in effect

Real-Time Properties column

"T" indicates track-based Real-Time Properties in effect

MIDI Real-Time Properties in an Instrument Track

 Track-based Real-Time Properties may be different for different edit Playlists. You will learn about using alternate Playlists in Module 8.

 Clips modified using clip-based real-time properties are marked with an "R" based upon the word "region". "Region" is a traditional term in Pro Tools versions up to version 10, where the term was changed to "clip."

The Real-Time Properties window provides additional options that are not available from the Real-Time Properties column in the Edit window.

Clip-Based Real-Time Properties

Clip-based real-time properties apply to a clip, or a selection of clips, and remain in effect even if a clip is moved to another MIDI or Instrument Track. Use clip-based properties to override the track-based properties, where necessary, or to apply different settings to different areas within a single track.

To add real-time properties to a clip:

1   Select the clip(s) you want to affect.

2   Choose EVENT > MIDI REAL-TIME PROPERTIES. Ensure that the APPLY TO: menu shows the selected clip(s) rather than a track.

3   Configure the settings in the Real-Time Properties window. If you play back the selection while adjusting the parameters, you can audition the changes as they are made.

4   When you are finished, close the window. You do not need to click a button to accept the changes, since they are applied in real time as you set each parameter.

 Do not click the WRITE TO CLIP *(or* WRITE TO TRACK*) button unless you want to apply changes permanently. This operation causes the changes to be written into the clip.*

The Real-Time Properties window offers an extended set of settings and parameters compared to the Track-based settings in the Edit window.

Real-Time Properties Settings

In the Pro Tools 110 course, we explored the Grid Quantize settings, but there are many more ways in which MIDI performances can be manipulated in real time. The MIDI Real-Time Properties are a slightly simplified subset of Pro Tools' Event Operations.

To access detailed parameters for a given type of Real-Time Property, click the expand/collapse triangle next to the Property type in the Real-Time Properties window.

Expand/collapse triangles

Quantize Real-Time Properties

Grid and Groove Quantize options are available from the Quantize pop-up menu. The options for Grid Quantize include % swing, tuplet, and grid offset settings, as well as settings to define a strength amount, an "include" range, and a randomize amount. For details on Grid Quantize Properties, see the Pro Tools 110 coursebook.

The Groove Quantize options available in the Real-Time Properties window are similar to those covered earlier in this module. These provide controls for setting the extent to which the groove's duration and velocities are applied, in addition to defining the strength amount, include range, and randomize amount.

To display the Groove Quantize options, select a groove template from the Quantize pop-up menu.

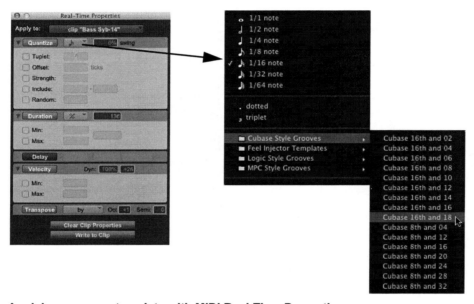

Applying a groove template with MIDI Real-Time Properties

- Duration, Velocity, and Strength: The DURATION and VELOCITY settings are identical to their counterparts in the Grid/Groove Quantize dialog box (without the sliders), influencing the durations and velocities of the MIDI notes, respectively, relative to the groove template. The STRENGTH setting is similar to the TIMING setting in the Grid/Groove Quantize dialog box, moving notes by a percentage towards the underlying template locations; however, the Strength Percent field only accepts values from 0 to 100%.

- Include: The Include settings cause Pro Tools to quantize only those notes that fall within the specified range of their counterparts in the groove template. The start and end fields accept values from 0 to 100%.

- Random: The RANDOM setting is identical to the RANDOMIZE setting in the Grid/Groove Quantize dialog box (without the slider), causing notes to be randomly moved earlier or later in time in relation to the groove's normal timing.

Duration Real-Time Properties

The Duration Real-Time Properties can be used to increase or decrease the length of MIDI notes in the selected clip(s) or track(s) by a fixed amount or by a percentage. This property is particularly useful for creating legato or staccato passages. To use Duration, select a Duration Mode from the pop-up menu and set the Amount and Min and Max options as needed.

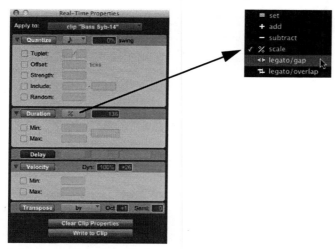

Selecting a Duration Mode

Delay Real-Time Properties

The Delay Real-Time Properties let you delay or advance all MIDI data in the selected clip(s) or track(s). Select "+" from the Delay Sign pop-up menu to delay MIDI data, or select "–" to advance MIDI data. Select ticks or ms from the Delay Units pop-up menu. Enter the Delay amount (or advance amount) in Tick or Millisecond values. Delay/advance is limited to a maximum of value of 2000 ms or 999 ticks.

Velocity Real-Time Properties

The Velocity Real-Time Properties let you change MIDI velocity values for the selected clip(s) or track(s) by a percentage or by a constant value. Enter a percentage value in the Dyn (Dynamics) field to scale velocity deviations relative to a median velocity of 64. You can enter an offset by adding (+) or subtracting (–) values between 1 and 127. You can also enter Minimum and Maximum Velocity value limits.

Transpose Real-Time Properties

The Transpose Real-Time Properties enable you to transpose MIDI notes in three different ways. You choose the type of transposition from the TRANSPOSE MODE pop-up menu (in either the Real-Time Properties column or the Real-Time Properties window).

- Transpose by: In this mode, every note is shifted up or down by the specified number of semitones and octaves.

- Tranpose to: In this mode, every note is changed to the exact note specified.

- Transpose in (key): In this mode, notes are moved in scale steps conforming to the key at that point in the session (as set in the Key Signature Ruler). You will learn more about transposing in key later in Module 6.

Making Sense of Transpose Interval Values

The 'Transpose By' Interval is measured in semitones, with 0 signifying no change. Thus a Transpose Interval of +2 equates to transposing up by a whole tone, and -12 equates to transposing down an octave.

The 'Transpose in' (in key) interval chosen will change the pitch in relation to scale steps. Therefore a Transpose interval of +2 equates to transposing up by a third (major or minor, depending on the key, +4 equates to transposing up a fifth, and -7 equates to transposing down an octave.

Writing Real-Time MIDI Properties

At any time, you can opt to make your Real-Time Properties permanent, processing the data in the clip in the same way as with the non-real-time Event Operations. You can write properties to a clip, a selection of clips, or all the clips in a track or multiple tracks.

To write Real-Time Properties to a track:

1   Select a track or multiple tracks containing Real-Time Properties.

2   Open the Real-Time Properties floating window (EVENT > MIDI REAL-TIME PROPERTIES).

3   Select the track(s) from the Real-Time Properties APPLY TO: pop-up menu, if not already selected.

4   Click the WRITE TO TRACK(S) button. The changes will be written into the MIDI notes on the selected tracks, and the Real-Time Properties window will clear.

To write Real-Time Properties to a clip:

1   Select one or more clips containing Real-Time Properties.

2   Open the Real-Time Properties floating window (EVENT > MIDI REAL-TIME PROPERTIES).

3   Select the clip(s) from the Real-Time Properties APPLY TO: pop-up menu, if not already selected.

4   Click the WRITE TO CLIP(S) button. The changes will be written into the MIDI notes in the selected clips, and the Real-Time Properties window will clear.

Introduction to the Score Editor

Whereas the MIDI Editor window can display notation in continuous lines alongside the session timeline, the Score Editor window allows you to view and edit MIDI tracks as notation in a more traditional page view. In the Score Editor window, you can edit, arrange, and print MIDI as notation. Whether you record, import, draw (with the Pencil tool), or Step Enter MIDI, the Score Editor will display MIDI notes in real-time.

The Score Editor Window

You can open and manage Score Editor windows in the same way as MIDI Editor windows; the main difference being that you can't dock a Score Editor into the Edit window. Just like with MIDI Editors, the targeted Score Editor displays the selected tracks shown in the Edit window, and you can show and hide tracks from the Score Editor's local Track List.

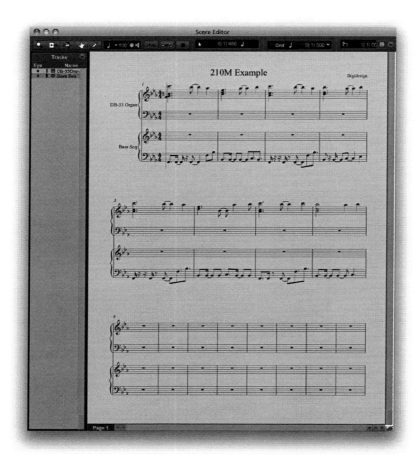

A Score Editor window with the same selection as the MIDI Editor earlier in the module

The Contents of the Score Editor Window

To open a Score Editor window:

1 [Optional] Make an Edit Selection through some MIDI / Instrument Tracks.

2 Choose WINDOW > SCORE EDITOR. The Score Editor window will open.

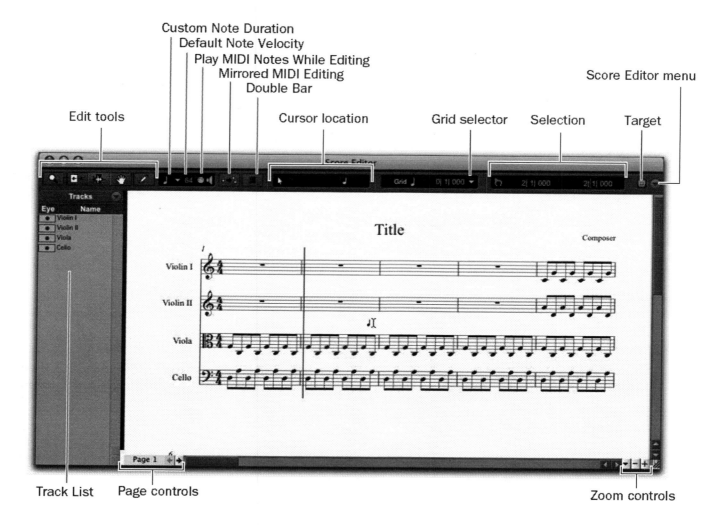

Adjusting the Appearance of Scores

Pro Tools provides a degree of control over how notes are transcribed and displayed in the Score Editor. This is useful both when editing and when setting up scores for printing.

Score Setup

The Score Setup dialog allows you to specify the main display settings for the score, such as the title and composer, and the staff spacing.

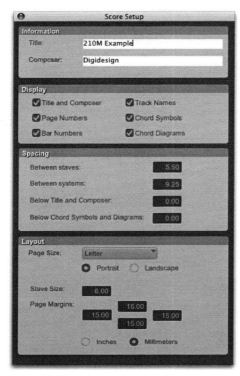

Score Settings

To open the Score Setup, do one of the following:

- Choose FILE > SCORE SETUP.

- From the Track List pop-up menu in the Score Editor window (or a MIDI Editor window when in Notation view), select SCORE SETUP.

- Right-click in the Score Editor window (or a MIDI Editor window when in Notation view) and select SCORE SETUP.

- Double-click the Title or Composer labels on the first page of the score.

Transcription Settings

You can adjust the way notes are transcribed using the Notation Display Track Settings window. Settings are made on a track-by-track basis, but some settings can be globalized.

To open the Notation Display Track settings do one of the following:

- From the Track List pop-up menu in the Score Editor, select NOTATION DISPLAY TRACK SETTINGS.
- Right-click in the Score Editor and select NOTATION DISPLAY TRACK SETTINGS.
- Double-click a Clef on a Staff.

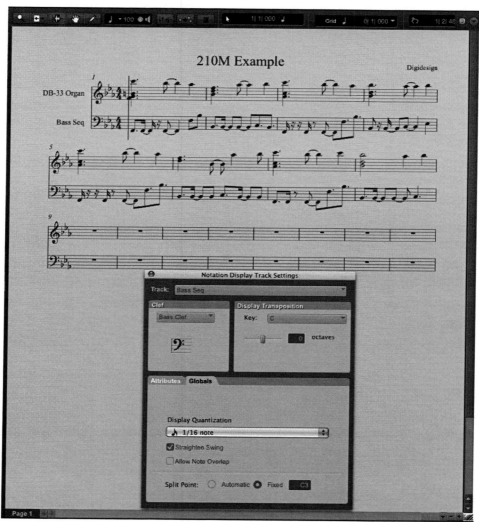

Track Display Settings

Clef

From the Clef pop-up menu, select the Clef you want for the selected track from the following options:

- Grand Staff
- Treble Clef
- Bass Clef
- Alto Clef
- Tenor Clef

In the previous image, space has been used efficiently by setting each part to a single staff.

Display Transposition

From the Key pop-up menu, select the key of Transposition for the track. For instruments that transpose from another octave, you can also adjust the Octave slider. For example, for a Bass Clarinet track, select the Key of B-flat and set the Octave slider to +1. This way, when you print the Bass Clarinet part, the player will be able to read the part and concert pitch will sound correctly a Major ninth below where the part is written.

Display Quantization

The DISPLAY QUANTIZATION setting lets you select the quantization grid for the display of MIDI notes in music notation. MIDI notes in Pro Tools still maintain their original start time and duration - this setting affects only what note values are displayed.

Straighten Swing

When enabled, the STRAIGHTEN SWING option causes "swung" notes to be displayed as straight notation.

Allow Note Overlap

When enabled, the ALLOW NOTE OVERLAP option allows for overlapping notes in the displayed notations. When it is disabled, notes that overlap as a result of legato playing are displayed normally.

Split Point

When the Clef for the selected track is set to Grand Staff, the selected SPLIT POINT setting determines at which pitch the notes are placed in either the upper or lower staff of the Grand Staff.

- Automatic—When selected, Pro Tools splits notes between the upper and lower staves of the Grand Staff based on logical note groupings.
- Fixed—When selected, you can specify a particular pitch at which to split notes between the upper and lower staves of the Grand Staff.

Editing in the Score Window

Selecting Notes

You can use either the Note Selector tool or the Grabber tool to select notes on one or more staves:

Selecting Notes by dragging with the Note Selector (left) or marqueeing with the Grabber (right)

Note Selector

Use the Note Selector tool to select notes on one or more staves in the Score Editor window. Selected notes are highlighted in blue. Selected notes can be deleted, moved, transposed, and processed (using Event Operations).

 The Note Selector tool only makes object selections, not range selections. Because of this, some commands and operations that require a Timeline selection cannot be applied in the Score Editor window.

Grabber

Use the Grabber tool to select one or more notes.

Edit Tools

The Score Editor has the same basic Edit Tools as the Edit window, but with some behaviors specific to notation editing:

- Grabber—You can use the Grabber tool to move single notes, or all selected notes, to a different transposition or time location.

- Trimmer—The Trimmer tool lets you extend the duration of a note.

- Pencil—The Pencil lets you insert, select, move, or delete notes. The various Pencil tools differ in how they draw note durations, repeated notes, and velocities, functioning in similar fashion to drawing notes on tracks in Notes view in the Edit window.

Transposing Notes

You can use the Grabber tool or the Pencil tool to manually transpose a note up or down. You can also use the Transpose Event Operation (EVENT > EVENT OPERATIONS > TRANSPOSE) to transpose selected notes.

Transposing a single note with the Grabber (left) or a range of notes (right)

Moving Notes

You can use the Grabber tool to move selected notes from one time location to another time location on the same staff. When moving notes in the Score Editor, any subtle timing variations in the MIDI notes is maintained, i.e moving notes in the Score Editor does not snap them to the Bars/Beats grid.

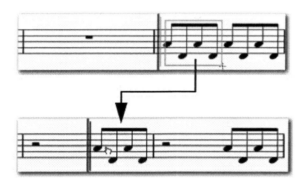

Moving a selected group of notes with the Grabber

Inserting Notes

Use the Pencil tool to manually insert notes in the Score Editor. When you insert a note, the Score Editor automatically places it on the Grid and creates rests where appropriate.

To manually insert a note:

1 Select the CUSTOM NOTE DURATION and DEFAULT NOTE ON VELOCITY.

Custom Note Duration Selector

Default Note On Velocity Selector

2 Select the Grid setting you want.

3 Click the Pencil tool and select Free Hand.

4 With the Free Hand Pencil tool, do any of the following:

- Single-click at the desired time location and pitch to enter a single note of the selected Custom Note Duration.

- Click at the desired time location and pitch and drag to the right to increase the duration of the note. Release the mouse when you reach the desired duration.

Printing Scores

Pro Tools lets you print the score from your Pro Tools session. Pro Tools provides WYSIWYG ("what you see is what you get") printing. Configure the Score Setup as desired and show or hide any MIDI and Instrument Tracks as desired. Only those tracks that are shown in the score will be printed.

To print the score from your Pro Tools session:

1 Open the Score Editor window and configure your score as desired.

2 Choose FILE > PRINT SCORE.

Press COMMAND+P *(Mac) or* CTRL+P *(Windows) to Print Score.*

Review Questions

1   What are some differences between Targeted and un-Targeted MIDI Editor windows? (See "Target" on page 89.)

2   How can you set which MIDI track is affected by the Pencil Tool in a MIDI Editor? (See "Track Edit Selector" on page 88.)

3   What is the difference between opening the MIDI Editor from the View menu (VIEW > OTHER DISPLAYS > MIDI EDITOR) and opening it from the Window menu (WINDOW > MIDI EDITOR)? (See "The MIDI Editor Window" on page 80.)

4   What are the two views available for displaying tracks in the notes pane of the MIDI Editor? (See "Tracks Display" on page 83.)

5   What is Groove Quantize? What are groove templates? (See "Groove Quantize" on page 89.)

6   When can Restore Performance be used to undo changes made to a MIDI performance? When can't it be used? (See "Restore Performance" on page 92.)

7   What is the difference between track-based Real-Time Properties and clip-based Real-Time Properties? (See "Real-Time MIDI Properties In Depth" on page 95.)

8   What is the main difference in the way notation is displayed in the Score Editor compared to the Notation View in the MIDI Editor? (See "Introduction to the Score Editor" on page 102.)

9   How can you set which kind of Staff a track is transcribed to in the Score Editor? (See "Transcription Settings" on page 105.)

10   What happens to the MIDI data in a track if you edit it in the Score Editor? (See "Introduction to the Score Editor" on page 102.)

11   Describe the various methods available for opening the Score Setup window. (See "Score Setup" on page 104.)

Exercise 4 Editing MIDI

This module will cover some of the features of the MIDI Editor window and Real-Time MIDI Properties.

Objectives:
- Program a MIDI sequence using the MIDI Editor window.

Approximate Completion Time: 40 minutes.

Introduction

In the last exercise, you worked with a Structure patch containing four string parts, with each part triggered by the same MIDI clip. In this exercise, you will use the MIDI Editor window to create separate MIDI clips for each string part. This will give you a chance to become familiar with the ways in which the MIDI Editor and main Edit windows interact. You'll also use Real-Time MIDI Properties to manipulate MIDI data, record the output of the string parts to audio, and print a final score.

Scenario

When the 210M song was being written, a single MIDI string part was created.

Your task is now to rearrange the single string part to play the four separate string parts in Structure.

Getting Started

Open your session from Exercise 3:

1   The starting point for this exercise is the session you saved in Exercise 3.

    – If you do not have a usable session from Exercise 3, a pre-prepared session for this exercise can be found in the 210M PT10 EXERCISE 4 folder, in the location specified by your instructor (such as Audio Drive: 210M PT10 Class Files: 210M PT10 Exercise 4: 210M Exercise 4.ptx).

2   If the Missing Files dialog box opens, choose Manually Find and Relink; the files are located in the 210M PT10 EXERCISE MASTER folder in the location specified by your instructor (such as Audio Drive: 210M PT10 Class Files: 210M PT10 Exercise Master).

3   Save the session to the location specified by your instructor, with the name <your initials>210M Exercise 4.ptx.

Re-familiarize

Make sure the parts still play back from Structure when you play MIDI notes from your keyboard. Remember to set the audio tracks you created to Input Monitor mode so you can hear the internally routed signals.

Assign the Structure parts to separate MIDI channels [Guided]

1   Click on the Structure plug-in to open the plug-in interface.

2   Set the string parts to the following MIDI channels:

  – Basses - A2

  – Celli - A3

  – Violas - A4

  – Violins - A5

3   Create four new MIDI tracks and name them M Basses, M Celli, M Violas, and M Violins. (The "M" is to denote that these are MIDI tracks.)

4   Set the outputs of the MIDI tracks to play the corresponding parts in Structure.

Create the First MIDI Clip [Guided]

1   Using the Grabber, double-click the Full Strings clip to open it in the MIDI Editor.

2   Use the Grabber to select all of the MIDI notes between C1 and C3. Choose Edit > Copy to copy the selected notes.

3   Select the M Basses track and click the Pencil column to the right of the M Basses track in the MIDI Editor's Tracks List. (This will direct all edit commands to the M Basses track.)

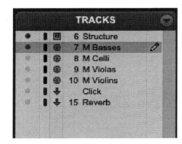

4   Choose Edit > Paste to paste the copied MIDI notes to the M Basses track.

5   Close the MIDI Editor and verify that a new MIDI clip has been created on the M Basses track containing the desired notes. Play back the session if desired to hear the result.

Use MIDI Real-Time Properties to modify a track [Guided]

1. Copy the newly created M Basses clip to the M Celli track.

2. Use MIDI Real-Time Properties on the M Celli track to transpose the clip up one octave.

3. Play back the session to hear the Basses and Celli together.

Use Select/Split Notes to edit MIDI notes [Guided]

1. Once again, use the Grabber to double-click the Full Strings clip to open it in the MIDI Editor.

2. Choose Event > Event Operations > Select/Split Notes.

3. In the Event Operations dialog, set the Pitch Criteria to Notes Between C3 & C4. Set the Action to Select notes. Click Apply.

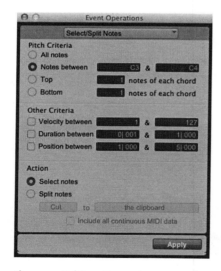

4. Choose Edit > Copy to copy the selected notes to the clipboard.

5. Select the M Violas track and click the Pencil column to the right of the M Violas track in the MIDI Editor's Tracks List.

6. Choose Edit > Paste to paste the copied MIDI notes to the M Violas track.

7. Close the MIDI Editor and verify that a new MIDI clip has been created on the M Violas track containing the desired notes.

8. Play back the session to hear the Basses, Celli, and Violas together.

Create the final MIDI clip [Challenge]

Task	Direction	Steps Used to Achieve Task
1	Return to the MIDI Editor window and select the notes between E4 and A5 using one of the techniques mentioned above. Copy these notes to the M Violins track.	

Record the loops as audio

When you've finished, you can try recording the string parts as audio into the tracks you created in Exercise 3.

Notice that the audio is recorded dry, i.e. pre any plug-ins or sends created on the audio tracks. After recording, the plug-ins and sends remain in the monitor path when you play the tracks back, so the sound is the same, and you still have the flexibility to change the plug-in settings or send levels.

[Optional] Print the string parts using the Score Editor

Task	Direction	Steps Used to Achieve Task
1	Use the Score Editor to hide the Structure part, change the individual string parts to the appropriate clefs, and print the score or create a PDF file.	

Module 5 Professional Audio Editing Techniques

This module looks at some expert methods for cleaning up and editing your audio.

Objectives:
- Adjust and edit loops on-the-fly with Dynamic Transport mode

- Fine-tune and customize fades

- Repair audio drop-outs and clicks using the Pencil Tool

- Use Beat Detective to correct the timing of multitrack drum recordings

Introduction

When composing and recording in Pro Tools, editing tasks tend to fall into two distinct categories. First, there's the cleaning up of individual recordings and clips; then there are larger scale arrangement edits. This module looks at the first of these families of tasks (large-scale editing will be explored in Module 7).

Editing with Dynamic Transport Mode

Occasionally, you will need to set up a playback time range or loop, make edits without losing this loop, and also control where playback starts from. Dynamic Transport is designed to enhance these workflows.

Example Workflow: Using Dynamic Transport with a Loop

Suppose that you would like to cut a 2-bar loop from a drum track and use it in your song. First you need to find the right start and end points for the loop to create a seamless transition. Using Loop Playback, you try listening to the segment repeatedly while adjusting your Timeline Selection Start and End Markers; however, you have to listen to the entire selection from start to end each time to hear the transition as it loops from the end of the selection back to the start, a process you find cumbersome and time consuming.

Dynamic Transport enables you to position your Play Start marker flexibly, without disturbing the timeline selection. In this case, you could move the Play Start marker to just before the Timeline Selection End Marker and begin playback from that point as often as needed. Playback starts at the Play Start Marker and continues across the loop point through the loop start, allowing you to easily audition the transition while fine-tuning your selection.

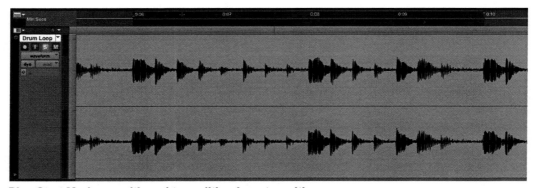

Play Start Marker positioned to audition loop transition

Next, suppose that after defining the selection, you decide to make an edit by copying the first kick and repeating it at another point in the loop. With Dynamic Transport active, since it automatically unlinks the edit and timeline selections, you can perform the edit without losing the playback loop. You can also reposition the play marker to the point you are working on.

 Activating Dynamic Transport will automatically unlink your edit and timeline selections. Upon exiting Dynamic Transport, this link will be re-established if the edit and timeline selections were linked before activating Dynamic Transport.

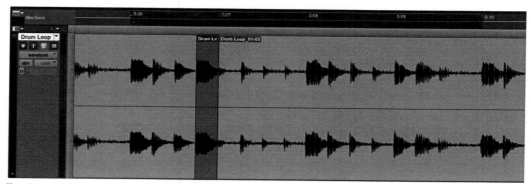

Further edits can be made without losing the playback range

Once you are satisfied with the edit, you can copy the Timeline selection to the Edit selection (EDIT > SELECTION > CHANGE EDIT TO MATCH TIMELINE), Separate the 2 bar drum loop with COMMAND+E (Mac) or CTRL+E (Windows), Group the selection (CLIP > GROUP) if necessary, and re-use it in your song as desired.

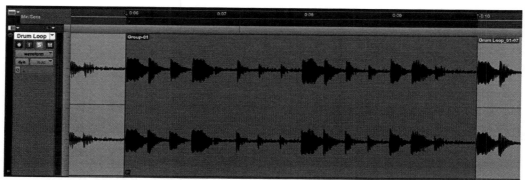

The new loop has been cut and Clip Grouped

Editing On-the-Fly

Pro Tools lets you perform many editing tasks while the session plays, enabling you to modify and edit a session interactively, and hearing the changes as you make them. You'll find many instances where you can use this capability to increase your productivity when working with a session.

Following are just a few examples of edits and related functions that can be performed while your tracks loop or play:

- Select audio or MIDI on a track or multiple tracks using the Selector or Grabber tools
- Adjust the Edit Selection Start or End Marker locations (with LINK TIMELINE AND EDIT SELECTION disabled)
- Capture, separate, loop, and trim clips
- Place, spot, or rearrange clips
- Add fades or crossfades to audio clips
- Transpose, quantize (including Groove Quantize), and otherwise modify MIDI tracks

- Nudge audio or MIDI clips

- Audition different playlists

- Adjust or scale automation data

- Process audio with an AudioSuite plug-in

- Process audio with Elastic Audio

These changes can be made without interrupting playback. However, if you make a change that affects a clip that is currently playing, you may experience a short update delay before you hear the change take effect.

Pro Tools also allows you to make on-the-fly changes that affect playback, such as adjusting Timeline selection boundaries or repositioning the Play Start Marker in Dynamic Transport mode. These changes will result in a brief interruption in playback and may cause playback to restart from the play start location, depending on the change and the transport mode in effect.

Customizing Fades

In this section, we look at ways to get the most out of fades. The fundamental purposes and techniques for creating and using fades have been discussed in previous Pro Tools courses. Here you will learn how to customize fades to get exactly the results you require.

Editing Fades

Some of the ways fades are created (such as using the Command Focus keys or the Smart Tool) apply default fade types. The defaults may be fine for many purposes, but you will also encounter times when you need to tweak a fade to make it sound exactly as you wish. Pro Tools provides several ways that you can edit and modify existing fades.

Changing a Fade

Two common ways to change an existing fade are to modify the fade curve and to modify the fade length. Both are simple operations.

To modify the fade curve:

1 Double-click the fade graphic attached to the clip on the track using the GRABBER tool. The Fades dialog box will appear, displaying the current fade type and parameters.

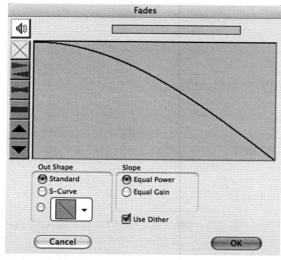

Fades dialog box

2 Do one of the following:

– Select the Standard or S-Curve option and customize the fade shape as needed by clicking and dragging to the left or right on the graph display.

– Select a new default fade curve from the fade shape pop-up menu (directly below the S-Curve radio button).

3 Click OK to close the dialog box. The original fade curve will be replaced by the new fade.

To modify the length of a fade:

- Click with the TRIM tool on the end or beginning of the fade that you wish to adjust, and drag with the mouse. You can watch the Start, End, and Length edit selection indicator boxes change as you trim as a guide to the size of your fade.

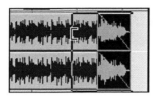

Trimming a fade

- The fade length will adjust accordingly when you release the mouse button.

 Trimming the outer edge of a fade in Shuffle mode will affect the sync and posi-tion of other clips on the track, just as regular trimming in Shuffle mode does.

Deleting Fades

As discussed in the Pro Tools 110 book, you can delete fades that have been applied to a clip without affecting the underlying clip. To delete a single fade, select a fade graphic in an audio track with the GRABBER tool and press DELETE or BACKSPACE on the keyboard. The fade will be deleted, leaving the original clip unchanged and extending up to the point the fade ended.

To delete one or more fades simultaneously, select the clip or range of clips that contain fades with the SELECTOR or GRABBER tool and choose EDIT > FADES > DELETE. The fades will be deleted, leaving the original clips unchanged.

Customizing Crossfades

Crossfades are more likely to need special attention than basic fade-ins and fade-outs. Some material can be difficult to fade transparently, and you may need to try several different fade lengths and shapes. Crossfades are most commonly used to smooth the transition between recordings of the same source, for example when piecing together several takes. However, they can also be used in other ways as well - to join together disparate material for special effects, for sound design, or to blend parts or whole songs together.

In this section, we follow the process that you might use to clean up the composite performance from Module 2. This is a typical editing scenario for a Pro Tools music session, and it highlights several editing concepts.

Example: Tidying up a Comped Recording

The following screenshot is an example of a finished comp from the Loop Recording section in Module 2. It comprises several clips selected from multiple record passes. At the moment, the edits are rough, with no fades.

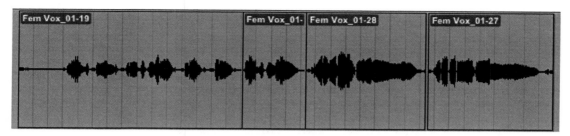

The following sections describe scenarios that arise while attempting to smooth the edits between the different sections.

Equal Power vs Equal Gain

The following screenshot shows a simple fade applied to the first transition of the composite performance. This was a default fade, created with the Smart Tool. The fade shape indicates that this particular Pro Tools system has the Equal Power fade option enabled for the default fade in the Preferences.

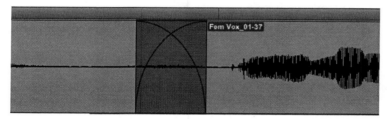

Equal Power Crossfade

Equal Power crossfades tend to produce an even level across transitions where the two sections of audio to be crossfaded audio are not in phase with each other. However, sometimes, as you can see in this waveform, this can produce a boost in level. In these cases, you may need to double-click the fade to open the Fade Editor and change the Link setting:

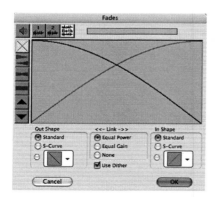 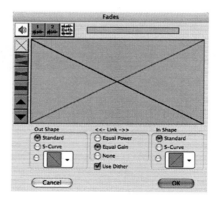

Equal Power (Left) and Equal Gain (Right) Crossfade links in the Fade Editor

Gaps and Double Breaths

A composite performance often has gaps between some clips. Typically these are smoothed using a combination of trimming and crossfading.

The following screenshots shows the boundary between the last two clips in the example composite:

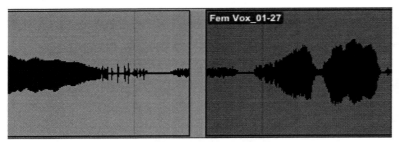

Gap between two parts of the composite performance

In the next screen, the gap has been closed by Trimming the incoming clip to meet the edge of the outgoing clip. By holding down the CONTROL key (Mac) or START key (Windows) while using the Trimmer tool, trimming will stop when you reach another clip boundary.

Gap closed by trimming.

Unfortunately, a common problem has been encountered that is unlikely to be solved by crossfading. In both takes the singer was taking a breath at the location of this transition. This will be clearly heard as two different breaths butted together. The solution is to re-trim the transition so that a complete breath is revealed from one of the takes.

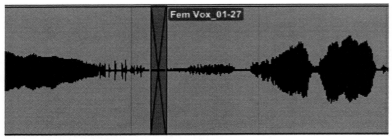

Transition point trimmed and faded

In the previous picture, the transition point has been moved slightly earlier, and a crossfade has been applied. If the transition point needs adjusting again, you can simply click and drag the crossfade left or right. When no crossfade has been applied, you can hold down the Command key (Mac) or Ctrl key (Windows) while using the Trim tool; trimming will operate on both boundaries of overlapping clips, maintaining a gapless edit in this situation.

Custom Fade Shapes

The following picture shows a problematic edit, caused by cutting between vocal takes in the middle of a line.

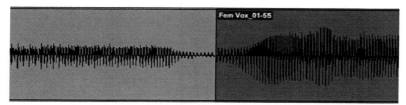

A hard transition between takes.

A simple fade shape may not produce a satisfactory result here. In the image below, a default fade has been applied, but this does not result in a natural sounding performance.

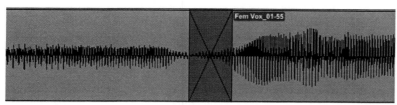

Default Fade

In this situation you can try creating a custom transition in the Fade Editor. There are two different customizations you can make: adjusting the fade center point, and adjusting the in and out fade shapes independently.

To adjust the center-point of a fade:

1   Double-click the fade with the Grabber tool to open the Fade Editor.

2   Click and drag left or right in the main fade shape display.

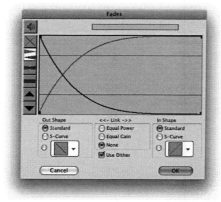

Center-point of fade moved earlier

To adjust the in and out slopes independently:

1 Double-click the fade with the Grabber tool to open the Fade Editor.

2 Set the Link option to NONE.

3 Click and drag the black squares that appear at the ends of the fade graphs.

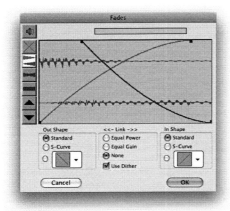

Independent in and out fades

The screenshot above shows the custom fade that created a smooth and natural sounding transition in the vocal composite example. This crossfade combines a fast fade-out with a slower fade-in.

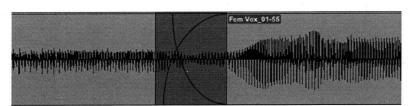

The custom fade in the Edit Window.

Using the Pencil Tool for Waveform Repair

The Pencil tool allows you to "redraw" waveform data. This tool is commonly used to repair a pop or click in an audio file. A pop or click appears as a sudden sharp spike in a waveform.

 The Pencil tool is a destructive editing tool that modifies the audio file on disk, and only becomes active in the waveform display when the Edit window is zoomed in to the sample level. It should be used with caution.

Although you can Undo a Pencil tool edit (up to 32 levels of undo, as per Pro Tools' Preference dialog box settings), it is recommended that you create a backup copy of the target audio before using the Pencil tool. You can do this by using the AudioSuite Duplicate plug-in or by using the Consolidate Clip command.

To make a backup copy of an audio clip:

1 Select the source clip in the track's playlist.

2 Choose AUDIOSUITE > OTHER > DUPLICATE. The Duplicate plug-in window will open.

3 In the AudioSuite window, make sure that PLAYLIST is selected in the Selection Reference pop-up, and that the USE IN PLAYLIST button is enabled.

4 Click the PROCESS button.

– The AudioSuite Duplicate plug-in creates a new audio file that is a duplicate of the original. The duplicate replaces the original on the track, and it is automatically named with the clip name and the suffix "DUPL." Your original file is preserved on disk and in the Clip List so that you can return to it, if needed.

To edit an audio waveform with the Pencil tool:

1 Locate and zoom in on the area you want to edit. A good technique for doing this is to use the Scrubber to zero in on the click, then zoom in where the Scrubber drops the edit cursor (the preference setting for Edit Insertion Follows Scrub/Shuttle must be enabled).

2 Adjust the Track Height, as necessary, to edit the waveform with greater precision.

3 Zoom in so that the click is large on the screen, while still allowing you to see the shape of the waveform around it.

4 Select the (Freehand) Pencil tool.

Pencil Tool

5 Carefully draw with the Pencil by dragging over the desired area of the waveform.

— Don't over-edit or the results may be undesirable. You can use the Undo command to undo your previous edit.

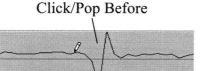

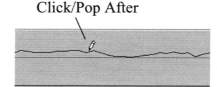

Removing Click/Pop with Pencil Tool

    For best results, try to limit editing to smoothing over a very small problem area, and keep the fixes in character with the shape of the surrounding waveform.

Introduction to Beat Detective

Beat Detective is a powerful tool for analyzing, editing, and manipulating audio or MIDI tracks that have an inherent rhythmic character.

Beat Detective analyzes an audio or MIDI selection, identifies its peak transients or accented notes, and generates beat triggers based on the detected peak transients or MIDI notes. Using these beat triggers, Beat Detective can do the following:

- **Extract a tempo map from freely recorded audio or MIDI**—Beat Detective can convert beat triggers to Bar|Beat Markers, making it possible to extract a tempo map from audio that was recorded without a click or MIDI that was recorded without reference to the session tempo.

- Create Groove Templates—Beat Detective can extract groove templates from an audio or MIDI performance. Groove Templates can be used to apply the feel of the captured performance to other audio selections or MIDI data.

- Conform audio to a tempo map—By first separating audio into smaller clips, Beat Detective can conform a performance to align with a timing grid. Beat Detective can conform audio recorded audio to follow the session's tempo map, improving the timing of individual drum hits and quantizing them to the uniform tempo of the session

- Smooth edits—Beat Detective's Edit Smoothing can be used to automatically clean up tracks that contain many clips requiring trimming and crossfading, effectively removing the gaps of silence between the clips.

ADDITIONAL APPLICATIONS FOR BEAT DETECTIVE

Although Beat Detective is most commonly used for tightening up drums and conforming performances across a song to match rhythmically, it can also be used for other creative purposes. Some examples include the following:

Loop matching—You can use the tempo extraction and conforming capabilities of Beat Detective on a small scale to capture the tempo or groove of one loop and apply it to another. This allows you to import loops or audio clips from different recordings and beat-match them with one another.

Creating remixes—You can use tempo extraction and conforming in a more radical way to conform the audio or MIDI material for an entire song to new tempos or grooves, creating a completely different feel for the song.

Creating Tick-based material—By slicing a rhythmic audio recording into individual beats and sub-beats, a performance can become independent of its original tempo. When placed on Tick-based tracks, the performance will follow tempo changes. By combing the slices into clip groups, you can work with them as a single entity while retaining the "elasticity" of the selection.

Beat Detective Overview

Beat Detective is most effective with audio or MIDI material that has clear attack transients or accent patterns, such as drums, guitar, or bass. Beat Detective will be less successful with audio material that has soft attacks, or legato phrasing, or widely varying tempos and is typically not well suited for working with strings or vocals.

Beat Detective can work with selections on multichannel tracks and with selections across multiple tracks. This allows Beat Detective to generate a set of trigger points based on the accumulated information in different audio or MIDI clips, such as from drum parts spanning multiple tracks.

To use Beat Detective effectively, you need to become familiar with the user interface in the Beat Detective window, understand the operational modes available in Beat Detective, and understand the general steps involved in a typical Beat Detective workflow.

RAM REQUIREMENTS FOR BEAT DETECTIVE

Beat Detective operations can require a large amount of RAM, especially when working with multiple tracks and lengthy selections.

If you begin to experience slow Beat Detective response, your computer may need more RAM. If increasing your RAM is not an option, the following work-arounds can help:

- Work with short selections on individual tracks, applying Beat Detective multiple times, rather working with a long selection or a selection across multiple tracks and applying Beat Detective only once.

- Set the Editing preference for Levels of Undo to a smaller value. Memory-intensive editing operations, such as Edit Smoothing (audio only), can consume a large amount of memory in the Undo queue.

The Beat Detective Window

The Beat Detective window provides all the controls for applying Beat Detective workflows in any of its five modes. The top of the window is divided into three main sections. On the left is the Operation section, where you select the Beat Detective mode for the operation you wish to perform. In the middle is the Selection section, where you define the characteristics of your selection. The section on the right changes dynamically between Detection, Conform, or Smoothing parameters, depending on the Operation mode selected.

At the bottom of the window is an information/navigation section that displays information about the currently active mode and provides a progress bar and navigational scroll buttons. The bottom right corner has the main button for applying the selected action for each mode.

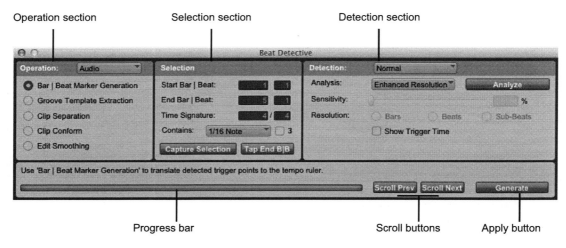

Beat Detective window

To open the Beat Detective window:

- Choose EVENT > BEAT DETECTIVE.

  – or –

- Press COMMAND+[8] (Mac) or CTRL+[8] (Windows) on the numeric keypad.

  Beat Detective will open in a floating window that can be left open while working. This window allows you to adjust the controls in real time during playback, while viewing the beat triggers that appear in your selection in the Edit window.

Beat Detective Modes

Beat Detective has five modes, accessed separately with the buttons in the Operation section of the window. These modes correspond to the workflows that Beat Detective can be used for: generating Bar|Beat markers, extracting a tempo map or groove template, separating clips, conforming clips, and smoothing edits by trimming and crossfading.

One of the first three modes is typically selected for the initial operation, based on the intended result. The last two modes are generally used as secondary operations, following a Clip Separation pass.

- **Bar|Beat Marker Generation.** This mode generates Bar|Beat Markers corresponding to the transients detected in an audio or MIDI selection. In this mode, Beat Detective creates a tempo map from your selection and applies it to your session.

- **Groove Template Extraction.** This mode analyzes timing, amplitude, and velocity information from selected audio and MIDI data, extrapolates rhythmic and dynamic values, and saves them either to the Groove Clipboard or to disk as a DigiGroove template file.

- **Clip Separation (Audio Only).** This mode separates the selection into new audio clips based on transients detected in the selection. In this mode, Beat Detective functions similar to the SEPARATE AT commands, but with greater control and precision, creating clips that are metrically significant based on the rhythmic content of the audio.

- **Clip Conform (Audio Only).** Conforms all separated audio clips within a selection to the current tempo map or selected groove template. This mode is typically used in a second Beat Detective pass, following a Clip Separation pass.

- **Edit Smoothing (Audio Only).** Fills the gaps between audio clips or slices by automatically trimming them and optionally inserting crossfades. This mode is often used to smooth the edits after Clip Separation and Clip Conform passes.

 All five Beat Detective modes can be used for Audio. Only the first two modes are available for working with MIDI data.

Using Beat Detective to Clean Up Drums

This section describes the basic steps involved with using Beat Detective to improve the timing of a drum performance and align individual hits closer to the grid. For best results, the performance should already be close to the grid (i.e., following the session tempo map). Where this is not the case, the Identify Beat command can be used to match the session to the performance tempo or the Bar|Beat Marker Generation operation can be used to establish a basic tempo map.

For the purpose of this discussion, we will assume the drums were recorded to a click and generally follow the session tempo. Our objective will be to improve the timing of individual drum hits.

Step 1: Defining the Selection

The first step in using Beat Detective is to define a selection of audio material that you want to analyze. The best results are generally obtained by working in sections, analyzing and correcting a number of bars at a time.

For Beat Detective to correctly analyze a performance, it's very important that the length and meter of the selection be defined correctly. Typically, the selection should start on a downbeat and extend across an exact number of bars and beats in the source material. The selection cannot contain any meter or tempo changes.

MAKING A SOLID SELECTION FOR BEAT DETECTIVE

The way you make your selection will vary depending on your purpose and whether or not the existing material aligns with the session tempo (bars and beats).

For most material, select an exact number of bars based on the recording (use Slip mode to adjust the selection freely). Audition the selection using Loop Playback/Dynamic Transport mode to ensure that you have an exact number of bars and beats and to verify that the selection's start and end points fall cleanly on the beat as you hear it (don't necessarily go by the timeline selection as your guide). This option applies even when the audio has been recorded to a click, as any slight variations in timing during a recorded performance could cause the audio to deviate from the session Grid.

If the target audio matches the session tempo and aligns exactly with the Grid at its start and end points, select an exact number of bars according to the Bar|Beat ruler (using Grid mode). This option would apply in select cases only, such as when the subject audio has been used to generate the session tempo map.

To define a selection for Beat Detective:

1   In the Edit window, select a range of material on the target track, ensuring that your selection starts on a down beat and extends across an exact number of bars and beats.

You can use the Tab to Transient feature to make sure the selection's start and end points fall cleanly on the beat and use Loop Playback to check the accuracy of your selection.

When working on a long recording, select a practical-sized portion and work in stages, addressing a few bars at a time. Depending on the complexity, selections of 8 to 16 bars may be appropriate.

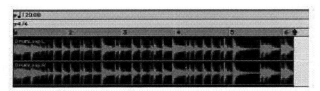

Making an audio selection for Beat Detective

2   In the Selection section of the Beat Detective window, enter a Time Signature for the selected material.

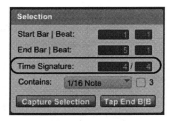

Beat Detective, Selection section

3   Click the CAPTURE SELECTION button to enter the start and end locations based on the Bar|Beat ruler. This operation does not require an exact match with the session Grid.

   If the selected material does not match the session tempo, enter Bar|Beat locations for the Start Bar|Beat and End Bar|Beat of your selection based your own musical judgment.

   You must define or capture the selection every time you make a new selection or change the tempo map.

4   To improve Beat Detective's accuracy in analyzing swung notes, select the smallest sub-division of the beat contained in the selection from the CONTAINS pop-up menu. Select the "3" checkbox to indicate a triplet modifier.

Step 2: Detecting Transients (Identifying Beat Triggers)

Once you've accurately defined a selection range, Beat Detective can generate markers, or *beat triggers*, based on the detected peak transients in the material. You will need to identify beat triggers whenever you wish to generate bar|beat markers, extract a groove template, or separate clips. For the purposes of cleaning up drum tracks, we will use the Separate Clips function, although any of the first three Operation modes can be selected while identifying beat triggers.

The range and type of transients that Beat Detective identifies as beat triggers can be adjusted with the settings in the Detection section of the window. You can use these settings to focus on critical bars, beats, and sub-beats in the material, while avoiding the non-rhythmic content.

Detection section of the Beat Detective window; Clip Separation options displayed

The Detection settings allow you to choose Normal or Collection mode from the Detection drop-down menu. Using Collection mode, you can analyze multiple tracks to get the relevant triggers from each track. You can then add each track's triggers to a trigger collection.

To detect beat triggers, you will always use Normal mode. You would switch to Collection mode only if/when you wished to add the detected beat triggers to a trigger collection.

   Using Collection mode is an advanced Beat Detective skill, and is explored in detail in the 310M course.

To create beat triggers for a selection:

1   Ensure that the appropriate Beat Detective mode is active and that your selection has been accurately defined.

2   In the Detection section of the window, select a detection algorithm from the Analysis pop-up menu:

 – **High Emphasis** — Works well for high frequency, inharmonic material, such as cymbals and hi-hats.

 – **Low Emphasis** — Works well for low frequency material, such as bass guitar and kick drum, as well as most harmonic/tonal material, such as piano or rhythm guitar.

 – **Enhanced Resolution** — Works well for a broad range of material, such as full mixes and loops. When available, this is the default analysis algorithm and is likely to produce the best results for the widest variety of audio material.

3   Click the ANALYZE button. Beat Detective will analyze the selection using the selected algorithm, and the Sensitivity slider and Resolution controls will become active.

4   Depending on the rhythmic content of the selection and the level of specificity that you wish to use when generating beat triggers, set the Resolution to BARS, BEATS, or SUB-BEATS.

 – Select BARS or BEATS to generate beat triggers at transients that represent the start of a bar or a beat location only, respectively.

 – Select SUB-BEATS to generate beat triggers at transients that represent any sub-division of the beat, as defined by the CONTAINS pop-up menu in the Selection section.

5   Adjust the Sensitivity slider until the desired beat triggers appear on the bars, beats, and sub-beats of the selection. Bar triggers are indicated with thick lines, beat triggers with medium lines, and sub-beat triggers with thin lines. The goal when adjusting the Sensitivity slider is to have musically significant transients marked with beat triggers, but to leave insignificant material unmarked.

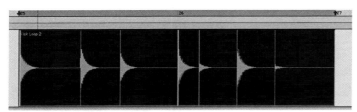

Beat triggers

Step 3: Editing Beat Triggers

While using Beat Detective, you will need to review the beat triggers in your track to determine if any must be deleted, moved, manually inserted, or otherwise modified.

Navigating Beat Triggers

When editing and verifying beat triggers, you will need to zoom in sufficiently to view the transients of individual beats and sub-beats, which can make it difficult to navigate through your selection. The scroll buttons at the bottom of the Beat Detective window solve this problem, allowing you to scroll the Edit window through the selection one beat trigger at a time.

Click the Scroll Next button to scroll the next beat trigger on the right into the center of the Edit window. Click the Scroll Prev button to scroll back to the previous beat trigger on the left.

Deleting Triggers

"False triggers," (those that do not represent an actual beat or sub-beat in the source material) may appear when raising the Sensitivity slider to detect low-level material. In these instances, you can manually delete these unwanted triggers.

To delete a beat trigger:

1   With the Beat Detective window still open, choose the Grabber tool in the Edit window.

2   Locate the trigger you want to delete. Transients for false triggers usually have smaller peaks than the other trigger points and typically fall between the sub-beats.

3   Option-click (Mac) or Alt-click (Windows) on the trigger with the Grabber tool to delete it. The trigger will disappear from the selection.

Moving Triggers

At times, you may want to adjust the placement of a beat trigger to allow for the attack of a transient or to compensate for a transient that is sightly ahead of or behind the beat. In such case, you can adjust the beat trigger to move it into the correct position.

To move a beat trigger:

1   With the Beat Detective window still open, choose the Grabber tool in the Edit window.

2   Click on the beat trigger you want to move and drag it to the left or right as needed.

Inserting Triggers

If an important beat or sub-beat is not detected, you can manually insert a beat trigger at the desired location, provided that existing beat triggers on either side can be sub-divided at the selected resolution.

To insert a beat trigger:

1   With the Beat Detective window still open, choose the Grabber tool in the Edit window.

2   Click in the selection where you want to insert the new trigger. A new trigger will appear. After clicking, you can drag left or right to adjust the trigger placement.

Promoting Beat Triggers

Occasionally when dealing with a section of audio, there a few particularly low-amplitude transients may be crucial to the character of a beat. Simply adjusting the Sensitivity slider is insufficient at this point, as in trying to mark these quiet but important hits, many false triggers would also be created.

While one option is to delete unwanted triggers, this can prove to be a difficult and time-consuming prospect. Promoting a beat trigger simplifies matters greatly.

To promote a beat trigger:

1 Set the Sensitivity slider so that the desired low-amplitude transient is marked.

2 Holding the Command (Mac) or CTRL (PC) key, click on the beat trigger that you want to keep. You'll note that when this modifier key is held, a small upward-pointing arrow can be seen within the Grabber cursor.

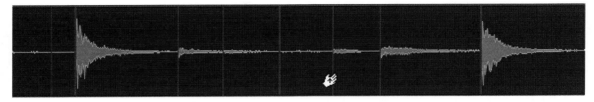

Promoting a Beat Trigger

3 After promoting the desired Beat Trigger(s), you can now lower the Sensitivity value without losing the promoted triggers, enabling you to keep only the Beat Triggers you need.

Changing the Value of a Beat Trigger

When Beat Detective marks transients, it assigns a Bar | Beat | Tick location for each Beat Trigger, based on it's analysis and your settings. You can see these locations by clicking the "Show Trigger Time" check box in Beat Detective's Detection section.

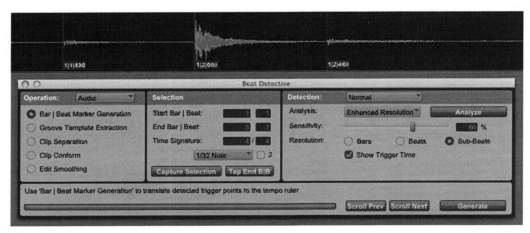

Showing Trigger Time in Beat Detective

Though these locations usually reflect a correct analysis of the selected material, but occasionally you may disagree with the location assigned by Beat Detective. Fortunately, changing the value of a Beat Trigger is a simple matter:

To change the value of a Beat Trigger:

1   Using the Grabber tool, double-click on the Beat Trigger that you want to change. The Identify Trigger dialog box will appear.

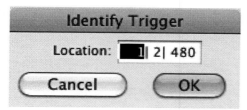

The Identify Trigger dialog box

2   Enter the value that the trigger should actually be.

3   Click the OK button. The Identify Trigger dialog box will close and your changed value will be applied. Note that the position of the Beat Trigger will remain unchanged.

Step 4: Separating Clips

Once Beat Detective has accurately generated the appropriate beat triggers for your selection, the selection can be automatically separated into meaningful clips, or slices, based on the beat triggers. The newly separated clips can then later be conformed to the grid.

To separate clips with Beat Detective:

1   With the Beat Detective window open and beat triggers accurately defined, select the CLIP SEPARATION radio button in the Operation section, if not already selected.

2   Enter a TRIGGER PAD value between 0 and 50 ms to pad clip start points relative to the beat triggers.

The Trigger Pad places space between the clip start point and the clip sync point, thereby ensuring that the attack portion of the material remains intact.

3   Click the SEPARATE button. Clips will be separated based on the detected beat triggers.

When separating clips with Beat Detective, sync points are created at each beat trigger location. When conforming clips, the clip sync point (not the clip start point) determines where the clip is placed.

Step 5: Conforming Clips with Beat Detective

After clips have been separated with Beat Detective, the clip timing can be adjusted to match the session Grid or a groove template. This is similar to using the CLIP > QUANTIZE TO GRID command or the QUANTIZE function in the Event Operations window.

To conform clips to the Grid:

1   In the Beat Detective window, select the CLIP CONFORM radio button in the Operation section.

2   Verify that the Selection settings you used previously are still active in the Selection section.

3   Choose Standard from the Conform pop-up menu.

Conform section of the Beat Detective window; Standard Conform options displayed

4   To affect how strongly the clips are conformed, select the Strength option and specify a percentage value either by using the slider or by typing in a value.

Lower percentage values preserve the original feel of the clips. Higher percentage values align the clips more tightly to the Grid. Try starting with a Strength setting of 85-88 percent.

5   To affect which clips are conformed, select the Exclude Within option and specify a percentage value by using the slider or by typing in a value.

Lower percentage values realign clips that deviate slightly from the Grid without affecting those that are already very close to the Grid. This preserves some of the original feel while correcting more significant timing errors. Higher values allow greater deviation from the Grid, creating a looser feel.

Try starting with an Exclude Within setting of 10–15 percent. This will preserve the feel of clips that are close to the beat while correcting those that are noticeably off.

6   To achieve a swing feel for the conformed clips, select the Swing option and specify whether the swing is based on 8th or 16th notes; then specify a percentage value.

Smaller percentage values yield less swing, while larger percentage values yield more swing.

7   Click the Conform button to automatically conform all clips in the selection.

8   Audition the new conformed clips to confirm the results by pressing Play in the Transport window to play back the selection.

If necessary, select Edit > Undo and try a different set of Conform settings.

Instead of using a grid based on the session's tempo map, Groove Conform uses a grid based on a groove template.

To conform clips using Groove conform settings:

1   In the Beat Detective window, select the Clip Conform radio button in the Operation section.

2   Verify that the Selection settings you used previously are still active in the Selection section.

3 Select GROOVE from the Conform pop-up menu.

Groove template pop-up menu

Groove Conform options in the Beat Detective window

4 Select a Groove template from the Groove Template pop-up menu, or select the Groove Clipboard, if available. To view comments for the selected template, click the SHOW INFO button.

5 To modify how the clips are conformed to the groove template, select the TIMING option and specify a percentage value by adjusting the slider or by typing in a value.

EFFECTS OF TIMING PERCENTAGES

The Timing percentage affects how strongly your audio slices are pulled toward the grid pattern of the selected groove template. If no Timing percentage is specified, the slices will align 100% to the template grid. With the Timing percentage set to 0%, the slices will ignore the template grid.

Percentage values below 100% preserve some of the original feel of the performance (lower values conform less to the template; higher values conform more). Values above 100% move the slices beyond the template grid. With the slider set to 200%, clips move to twice the difference between their original clip location and the template grid This often has the effect of exaggerating the character of the groove template.

For example, if a note exists at Bar 1|1|060 and the corresponding template event is at 1|1|073, a Timing value of 100% would shift the note to 1|1|073; a Timing value of 200% would shift the note to 1|1|086, overemphasizing the effect of the template.

6 If desired, enable the PRE-PROCESS USING STANDARD CONFORM option. With this option enabled, Beat Detective conforms clips to the current Standard Conform settings before applying the groove template. This sometimes leads to better results by ensuring that the performance is accurately mapped to the correct bars, beats, and sub-beats before the groove template is applied.

7 Click the CONFORM button to automatically conform all clips in the selection.

8 Audition the new conformed clips to confirm the results by clicking PLAY in the Transport window.

9 If necessary, select EDIT > UNDO, and repeat these steps trying a different groove template or different Groove Conform settings.

Step 6 (Optional): Smoothing Edits with Beat Detective

After clips are conformed, you may have gaps between the clips. These gaps can cause the material to sound unnatural on playback.

Beat Detective can automatically fill the gaps between clips and add crossfades. It does this by trimming out the start and end points of each clip. You can even use Beat Detective Edit Smoothing on tracks that were not conformed with Beat Detective, potentially saving many hours of editing.

 Another good application for Edit Smoothing is to fill gaps between clips on tick-based audio tracks after the session tempo has been decreased.

Smoothing options in the Beat Detective window

To use Edit Smoothing on clips in a track:

1   In the Beat Detective window, select Edit Smoothing in the Operation section.

2   Make sure the clips to be smoothed are selected in the Edit window.

    After conforming clips, you may need to adjust the Edit selection to encompass the range of conformed audio clips. (Conforming sometimes causes clips to move outside of the Edit selection.)

3   In the Smoothing section of the window, do one of the following:

    – Select the Fill Gaps option to trim clip start and end points so that the gaps between clips are filled.

    – Select the Fill And Crossfade option and specify a crossfade length to trim clip start and end points and automatically add a pre-fade directly before each clip start point. This can often remedy any clicks or pops that arise as a by-product of the movement of clips.

4   Click the Smooth button to trim the selected clips.

5   Audition the change to confirm the results by clicking Play in the Transport window.

    If necessary, select Edit > Undo and adjust the Crossfade Length.

Step 7 (Optional): Consolidating Clips after Edit Smoothing

The process of separating, conforming, and smoothing with Beat Detective can leave tracks with many clips and many crossfades. If you are working with multiple tracks, the density of these edits could lead to system performance problems.

Once you are satisfied with the results from Beat Detective, you can consolidate the clips by choosing EDIT > CONSOLIDATE or typing OPTION+SHIFT+3 (Mac) or ALT+SHIFT+3 (Windows). This command writes a single rendered audio file for each track over the entire selection, making it easier for Pro Tools to play back.

Using Beat Detective for MIDI Analysis

Beat Detective's MIDI analysis lets you use MIDI tracks to generate tempo and groove information. Groove information generated from MIDI is interchangeable with groove information generated from audio, meaning that you can apply MIDI generated grooves to audio material or vice versa.

MIDI analysis works in the following Beat Detective modes:

- **Bar|Beat Marker Generation**—This mode generates Bar|Beat Markers corresponding to the location of notes and chords in MIDI selections.

- **Groove Template Extraction**—This mode extracts the rhythmic and dynamic information from MIDI data and allows you to save this information to the Groove Clipboard or a Groove template file.

MIDI Analysis Workflow

The basic workflow for working with MIDI is the same as for working with audio. In the following example, a MIDI selection is used to create a groove template.

To extract a groove template from a MIDI selection:

1   In the EDIT window, set the MIDI track you wish to use to NOTES view.

2   Make a selection across a range of MIDI data. Make certain that the selection start and end points are at musically relevant locations, i.e. barlines/down beats.

3   Choose EVENT > BEAT DETECTIVE.

4   Select MIDI from the Operation pop-up menu.

5   Select GROOVE TEMPLATE EXTRACTION from the options in the Operation section.

6   Configure the Selection parameters as described earlier in this module.

7   In the Detection section, select a MIDI chord recognition algorithm from the Analysis pop-up menu. See "MIDI Chord Recognition" below for details. This setting is important only if the MIDI track contains chords.

8   Click the ANALYZE button. Beat Detective will analyze the selection using the selected algorithm, and the Sensitivity slider and Resolution controls will become active.

9   Set the RESOLUTION to Bars, Beats, or Sub-Beats to specify the level of granularity that you wish to use when generating beat triggers.

10 Adjust the SENSITIVITY slider until beat triggers appear on all the bars, beats, and sub-beats of the selection, as applicable. The slider will include notes based on their Velocity values.

11 Click the EXTRACT button, and choose whether to save the groove template to disk or to the clipboard.

MIDI Chord Recognition

Since MIDI notes in a chord may be played at slightly different moments, Beat Detective interprets notes that are close together (closer than half the value set in the SELECTION CONTAINS field) as a chord.

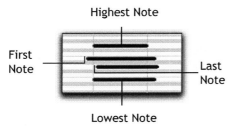

MIDI Chord Analysis

Beat Detective will use the criteria you set in the ANALYSIS pop-up menu to interpret the location of the beat in relation to the chord.

- **Last Note**—This option sets the beat trigger to the start of the last note played in the chord.

- **First Note**—This option sets the beat trigger to the start of the first note played in the chord.

- **Loudest Note**—This option sets the beat trigger to the start of the note in the chord played with the highest velocity.

- **Average Location**—This option sets the beat trigger to a point that represents the average between the start of the first note in the chord and the start of the last note in the chord.

- **Highest Note**—This option sets the beat trigger to the start of the highest note played in the chord.

- **Lowest Note**—This option sets the beat trigger to the start of the lowest note played in the chord.

Using Beat Detective to Create a Tempo Map

Beat Detective may not only be used to conform material on tracks to the session's timeline, but it can also be used to conform the session's timeline to match the content analyzed by Beat Detective. In other words, you can create a highly detailed tempo map based on the analysis of material in your session's tracks, allowing you to go further, and quantize (or conform) material on other tracks to match the feel of any desired track.

The process in creating this tempo map is largely similar to the steps you took to clean up drums, but with one important difference: After you've analyzed the desired selection, adjusted the sensitivity slider to mark significant transients, and tweaked any errant Beat Triggers, you will proceed to the following steps:

1 Select the Bar|Beat Marker Generation radio button in the Operation section of the Beat Detective window.

2 Click the Generate button in the lower right-hand corner of the Beat Detective window. If your session contains any tick-based tracks, the Realign Session dialog box will appear:

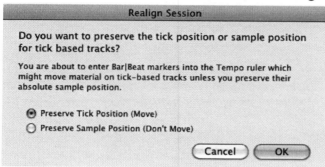

The Realign Session dialog box

3 Choose the appropriate radio button for your situation:

- Choose **Preserve Tick Position** to move data on tick-based tracks to match your new tempo changes. This is the choice to make if you want to have existing material (for example, MIDI notes) move into alignment with the section you analyzed with Beat Detective.

- Choose **Preserve Sample Position** to leave any data on tick-based tracks unchanged. With this radio button selected, the only change in your session will be the creation of a new Bar|Beat marker map in the Tempo ruler.

Creating a detailed tempo map in this way opens up many creative options in the use of Beat Detective. By creating a tempo map based on the analysis of a section (for example a section of audio drum tracks), you can now align other material to the new timeline by following the steps outlined in the "Using Beat Detective to Clean Up Drums" section earlier in this module.

Beat Detective for Multitrack Drums

In the previous section, you learned how the Separate and Conform operations can be used to chop up and quantize an audio recording. However, in many professional music production situations, the task required of Beat Detective is the tightening of drum performances, which are often recorded with several mikes onto multiple tracks.

 There are effective variations on the workflow provided here. Your instructor may share some other tips and practices to help you reach your goal.

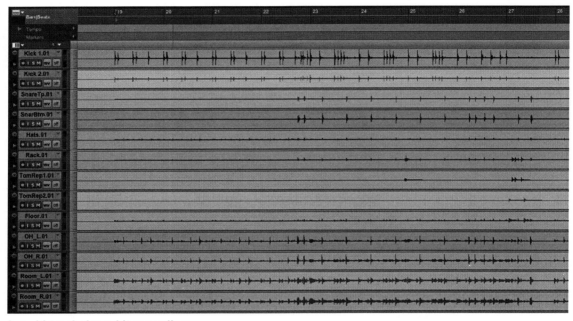

A multi-track drum-kit recording

This image shows a section of a typical multitrack drum kit recording. Beat Detective can be used to separate the tracks into short sections, and then conform (quantize) these sections to (or closer to) the Bars|Beats grid.

Summary of Key Concepts

Maintaining Phase

With any multi-mic recording, it's important to make sure the tracks maintain their time relationship with one another. Otherwise, delays between sounds picked up by more than one mic may give rise to phase cancellation problems.

This means that Beat Detective must apply the same cuts and time shifts across all drum tracks at once.

Applying Beat Triggers from One Track to Multiple Tracks

The top track in the previous image is the close mic on the kick drum, and the third track is the top mic on the snare. In some cases, these might be the only tracks you'll need to analyze to capture the character of a beat. Once you've analyzed these track and generated Beat Triggers, you can extend the edit selection to the other tracks and Separate all of them at the same places.

Using the Earliest Triggers

When applying triggers from one track to other tracks, it's important to use the earliest occasions of any particular hit. For example, the snare will appear in the close snare mics, the overheads, and the room mics, but there will be acoustic delay on the mics that are furthest away. If you choose a Beat Trigger on a later hit, the same hit on another track might get cut in half when you separate the clips. In this module, you will use the close kick mic and snare mic, which should avoid this problem.

Working in Sections

It is unwise to select the drums across the whole song, then try to analyze and separate them all in one go. The song will have varied sections, with different problems, and the best results will be obtained by breaking down the task into smaller sections. As a real-world example, the exercise following this module will focus on a 16-bar section.

Drum Editing Workflow

This is a simplified workflow, assuming no complications. We will assume that the drum performance matches the session tempo, although it may not be in perfect time with the grid. In the exercise you will attempt a more real-world scenario.

1. Duplicate the Playlists

In Module 7 you will learn how to use Pro Tools' Playlist functionality to create new or duplicated versions of the edit data within tracks. This allows you to edit tracks while keeping a 'safety' copy to return to if the results are unsatisfactory. It is recommended that you do this before working on drum tracks with Beat Detective.

To duplicate the drum playlists:

1 Group the drum tracks.

2 Click on the PLAYLIST SELECTOR (next to the track name) on any drum track and choose DUPLICATE.

- A copy of the playlists will appear for each of the drum tracks. You will be able to tell that you are working on a copy, as each track name will have a ".01" appended to the end.

3 Disable the drum Group.

 In Pro Tools 310M you will study the grouped Playlist feature further.

2. Select the area to work on

Make an edit selection across the tracks you wish to analyze (the kick and snare tracks in this example), and spanning the time range you will be working on first (e.g. 16 bars). The important part of this step is that you should select an exact number of bars, as they sound in the performance, rather than the session's Bar|Beat Grid. In other words, if the first kick sounds slightly before the beat (as displayed by the Pro Tools grid), you should select from where the kick actually is.

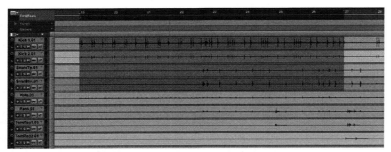 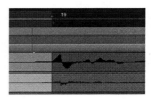

Edit Selection for first Beat Detective pass

3. Open Beat Detective and Select the Mode

1 Choose Event > Beat Detective to open the Beat Detective window.

2 Choose Clip Separation.

4. Capture the Selection and Specify the Meter

This step tells Beat Detective which bars you're working with, and what kind of beats are used in the performance.

To specify the selection and meter:

1 Enter the Time Signature if it's not 4/4.

2 Set the Contains field to describe the resolution you need to work with. For example, if the rhythm contains off-beat sixteenth notes, specify this so that the position of each drum hit is more likely to be assigned correctly. If the performance is played with a triplet feel, check the '3' box.

Click the Capture Selection button. The Start and End Bar|Beat fields will update to show the current edit selection. If the captured start and end locations are not on a bar boundary, you should manually enter the nearest bar.

5. Analyze the Tracks and Adjust Triggers Where Necessary

In this step you will use Beat Detective's transient analysis to detect beat triggers automatically, then, if necessary, make manual adjustments.

1   In the Detection section, start off by setting the Analysis mode to ENHANCED RESOLUTION. This offers the best detection for most material.

2   Click ANALYZE.

3   Adjust the Sensitivity slider until triggers appear for most or all of the kick and snare hits, with as few 'false positives' as possible.

4   Manually adjust, delete, or add triggers if necessary.

You will have a chance to refine these skills in the exercise.

6. Extend the Selection to all Tracks

When you are satisfied that the beat triggers represent the appropriate kick and snare hits on the selected tracks, extend the edit selection to all the drum tracks. If the tracks you analyzed are at the top of a group of drum tracks, the quickest way to extend the selection is to press SHIFT+; (semicolon) to add the tracks one at a time. It is important NOT to reanalyze newly added tracks, though Beat Detective will give you this option.

7. Separate and Conform the Drum Tracks

1   Click SEPARATE.

    – Pro Tools will separate each drum track at each beat trigger.

2   Click CLIP CONFORM to place Beat Detective into clip conform mode.

3   Adjust the Conform settings to determine how strongly the beats will be quantized, and whether they will be conformed with respect to the grid or to a groove template.

4   Click the CONFORM button.

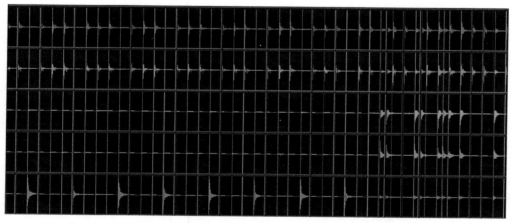

    – Pro Tools will move the clips based on the conform settings.

8. Smooth Edits

This optional step allows you to smooth the edits have been made by the Conform process.

1   Click EDIT SMOOTHING to place Beat Detective into edit smoothing mode.

2   Choose from FILL GAPS or FILL GAPS AND CROSSFADE. If choosing the latter, specify a crossfade length.

3   Click SMOOTH.

After auditioning the changes, you can select the next section and repeat the process.

Review Questions

1   What are some examples of operations that you can perform "on-the-fly" during playback? (See "Editing On-the-Fly" on page 121.)

2   What would cause a crossfade to produce a noticeable drop in volume across the fade? What can you do to correct the problem? (See "Equal Power vs Equal Gain" on page 125.)

3   In the Fade Editor window, how do you enable the black squares on the fade graphs that allow you to create a custom crossfade? (See "Custom Fade Shapes" on page 127.)

4   Why is it generally a good idea to Duplicate an audio file before editing the waveform with the Pencil Tool? (See "Using the Pencil Tool for Waveform Repair" on page 129.)

5   What are the five Operation modes in Beat Detective? Which can be used for both audio and MIDI material? Which can be used for audio only? (See "Beat Detective Modes" on page 132.)

6   What are the seven main steps involved in using Beat Detective to clean up a drum performance? (See "Using Beat Detective to Clean Up Drums" on page 133.)

7 What are beat triggers? What tool would you use to edit beat triggers? (See "Step 3: Editing Beat Triggers" on page 136.)

8 Describe some options for chord recognition when using Beat Detective in a MIDI analysis workflow. (See "MIDI Chord Recognition" on page 144.)

9 What are the steps that you would use to create Bar|Beat Markers based upon Beat Detective's analysis of a drum loop? (See "Using Beat Detective to Create a Tempo Map" on page 144.)

10 When editing multitrack drums, why should you make sure the same edits are applied to all tracks at once? (See "Maintaining Phase" on page 146.)

11 Can you think of any disadvantages of only using the kick and snare tracks when conforming drums with Beat Detective? (See "Applying Beat Triggers from One Track to Multiple Tracks" on page 147.)

Exercise 5 Audio Editing

Objectives:
- Tidy up the edit points in a vocal comp.
- Improve the timing of a multi-track drum recording using Beat Detective

Approximate Completion Time: 1 hour.

Introduction

This exercise is in two separate parts. Part A practices core editing skills using Trimming and Crossfades. Part B uses Beat Detective to fix a multi-track drum recording.

Part A - Edit Clean-Up

Scenario

The main vocal track in the 210M session has been comped from multiple takes. The producer has just roughly cut her favorite sections together, and has asked you to clean up the track by making sure all the edit points are smooth. You will use a combination of trimming and cross-fading to fix a number of problems identified in the track.

Getting Started

Open the session:

1   The session for this exercise is 210M PT10 Exercise 5a.ptx. The session file can be found in the 210M PT10 EXERCISE 5 folder, in the location specified by your instructor (such as Audio Drive: 210M PT10 Class Files: 210M PT10 Exercise 5: 210M PT10 Exercise 5a.ptx).

2   If the Missing Files dialog box opens, choose Manually Find and Relink; the files are located in the 210M PT10 EXERCISE MASTER folder in the location specified by your instructor (such as Audio Drive: 210M PT10 Class Files: 210M PT10 Exercise Master).

3   Save the session to the location specified by your instructor, with the name <your initials>210M Exercise 5a.ptx.

Once you've opened the session, you will see that the vocal comp track is enlarged and soloed. Eight markers have been placed in the Marker track to point out the problematic edits.

Identify and Fix the Rough Edits [Challenge] - 30 mins

Navigate to each of the 8 marker positions in the timeline and listen to the problems in the vocal track at those points. Identify what each problem is, and use a combination of trimming and fading to address the issues (as described in Module 5). Use the table below to record your assessment of the problems, and the steps you took to fix them. The first entry has been completed as an example. Take the steps indicated to fix problem 1, then work your way through the remaining 7 marker locations.

Marker	Problem	Steps to Fix
1	Edit point in the middle of two different breaths	Trimmed incoming clip earlier to reveal a single breath, then applied short crossfade.
2		
3		
4		
5		
6		
7		
8		

When finished, save and close the session. Then proceed to Part B, below.

Part B- Beat Detective - 30 minutes

Introduction

As a Pro Tools engineer, you may be called upon to take a drum performance and "lock it in" to the tempo of the song, or to match its groove to another rhythm track. Rock and pop music is often recorded to a click track, and many times the performance is not as "tight" as the producer would like. In this exercise, you will take 24 bars of unedited drums and use Beat Detective to lock them to a guide track of electronic percussion. Keep in mind that there are effective variations on the workflow provided here. Your instructor may share some other tips and practices to help you reach your goal.

Getting Started

Open the session:

1   The session for this part of the exercise is 210M PT10 Exercise 5b.ptx. The session file can be found in the 210M PT10 EXERCISE 5 folder, in the location specified by your instructor (such as Audio Drive: 210M PT10 Class Files: 210M PT10 Exercise 5: 210M PT10 Exercise 5b.ptx).

2   If the Missing Files dialog box opens, choose Manually Find and Relink; the files are located in the 210M PT10 EXERCISE MASTER folder in the location specified by your instructor (such as Audio Drive: 210M PT10 Class Files: 210M PT10 Exercise Master).

3   Save the session to the location specified by your instructor, with the name <your initials>210M Exercise 5b.ptx.

There are 5 drum tracks in the session, and a stereo track called "Groove" which will be your guide track for quantizing the live drums.

Extract the Groove from the Guide Track

The "Groove" track is closely matched to the tempo grid, and the producer would like the live drums to lock up to this track as closely as possible. Therefore, we must extract the groove from the "Groove" track and apply it to the live drums.

Capture the Groove track selection in Beat Detective:

1 Select the first clip on the "Groove" track.

2 Vertically zoom in to better see the transients on the quiet parts.

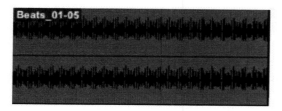

Vertical Zoom

3 Choose EVENT > BEAT DETECTIVE to open the Beat Detective window and choose GROOVE TEMPLATE EXTRACTION.

4 Ensure 1/16 NOTE appears in the resolution pop-up field.

– Since the selection contains sixteenth note rhythms, this setting will ensure that each drum hit is properly recognized.

5 Click the CAPTURE SELECTION button.

Analyze the selected tracks:

1 Click the ANALYZE button with Analysis set to High Emphasis.

2 Raise the SENSITIVITY to at least 15%.

    – Beat markers will appear before almost all of the hits on the selected tracks. Note that Enhanced Resolution is also an available Analysis option, based on the Elastic Audio algorithm. In this session, High Emphasis will likely provide the best results, but feel free to experiment.

Add beat triggers:

1 Zoom in on your selection. No matter how high you raise the sensitivity, you'll notice that the transients at bars 36|2|240 and 58|2|240 are not being recognized. You will need to manually add beat triggers at these points.

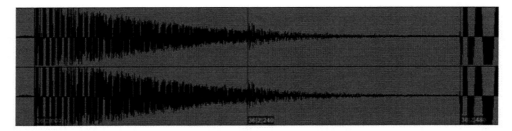

2 Using the GRABBER TOOL, click at the beginning of the transients at each of the locations mentioned above.

Extract the Groove:

1   Click EXTRACT.

    – Pro Tools will display a dialog box asking you how to save the groove:

2   Click SAVE TO GROOVE CLIPBOARD.

    – Saving to the clipboard is adequate in this case, since you will be using this groove shortly. You could also save the groove to disk for future use.

3   Hide the Beat Detective window: COMMAND+[8] (Mac) or CTRL+[8] (Windows).

Analyze the Kick and Snare Tracks

You are going to base your beat analysis around the kick, snare, and hi-hats. (Note, advanced analysis with Collection Mode is explored in the 310M class, for more complicated scenarios.)

It is always a good idea to perform your edits on a duplicate playlist. That way, you can quickly return to the original version by switching the playlists.

Create a duplicate playlist:

1   Enable the "Kit" edit group in the Edit window.

2   Click on the PLAYLIST SELECTOR (next to the track name) and choose DUPLICATE.

    – A copy of each playlist will appear for each of the drum tracks. Each track name will have a ".01" appended. Switch back to the original playlist in order to use the original track names (the .01 playlists will be your back-up).

3   Disable the "Kit" Edit Group in the Edit window.

Make the initial selection:

1 Make a selection from bar 35 to bar 59 across the kick drum track.

   – Listen to the drums solo'd; adjust the Music Reference track volume as necessary. Notice the first kick in the selection is slightly before the beat.

2 Put Pro Tools into Slip Mode.

3 With the GRABBER tool, drag the START PLAYBACK MARKER slightly to the left to include the transient. Adjust the END PLAYBACK MARKER similarly, this time to exclude the kick beat at bar 59, which is early.

4 Press OPTION+F (Mac) or ALT+F (Windows). The selection will zoom to fill the screen.

5 Using the Selector tool, COMMAND-CLICK (Mac) or CTRL-CLICK (Windows) on the Snare Top and Hi-Hat tracks to add them to the selection. You will use these tracks to analyze the Kick, Snare Top, and Hi-Hat tracks.

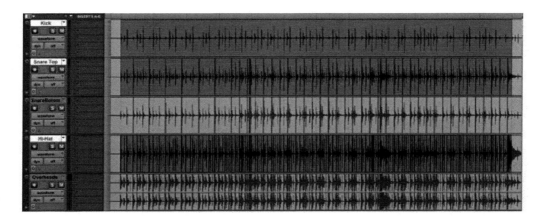

Capture the selection in Beat Detective:

1 Re-open the Beat Detective window and choose CLIP SEPARATION.

   – The Beat Detective selection should still be set to start at bar 35 and end at bar 59; keep this setting. Also keep the Resolution field at 1/16 NOTE.

2 Type 2 into the TRIGGER PAD field and click the ANALYZE button.

3 Set the SENSITIVITY to 15% (check the beat triggers).

4 Click the SHOW TRIGGER TIME check box to enable it.

   – Trigger Times will appear below each beat trigger.

5 Zoom in on the beat triggers.

6 Click the SCROLL NEXT button to scroll to the next beat trigger. Continue through the entire selection to make sure every proper transient is recognized.

   – You will notice extra triggers being detected from bars 53 to 55, due to a late hi-hat. These "false" triggers should be removed. Lowering the SENSITIVITY will eliminate too many "true" triggers, so manual removal is the best option in this scenario.

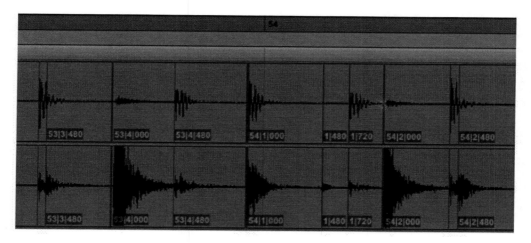

Remove beat triggers:

1 Make sure Pro Tools is in Slip mode.

2 Zoom in on the first doubled trigger at 53|3|480.

3 Using the GRABBER tool, hold down OPTION (Mac) or ALT (Windows) and click on the second trigger to remove it.

    – The first trigger is more desirable to keep because it is aligned with the beginning of the kick drum.

4 Perform the same operations at 54|2|480.

5 Remove any other false triggers (hint: last bar of selection).

    – The false triggers in bars 53 and 54 have forced the real triggers to have improper trigger times. You'll have to adjust these before conforming to avoid quantization errors. Often, you may not realize this until after attempting to Conform. In that case you would have to use the Undo History window and then proceed with the following steps.

Fix trigger times:

1 With the GRABBER tool, double-click the trigger at 53|3|240.

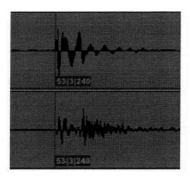

2 Change the LOCATION to read 53|3|480.

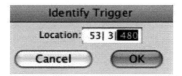

3 Also change the LOCATION of the trigger marked 54|2|240 to 54|2|480.

Separate, conform, and smooth the drum tracks:

1 To add the Overheads and Snare Bottom tracks to the selection, Command-click (Mac) or Ctrl-click (Windows) on each of these tracks.

2 Click SEPARATE.

– Pro Tools will separate each drum track at its beat triggers.

3 Click CLIP CONFORM to place Beat Detective into Clip Conform mode.

4 Choose Groove from the Conform menu and select Groove Clipboard from the secondary pop-up menu that appears below.

5 Click the CONFORM button.

– Pro Tools will move each of the clips to the closest groove value.

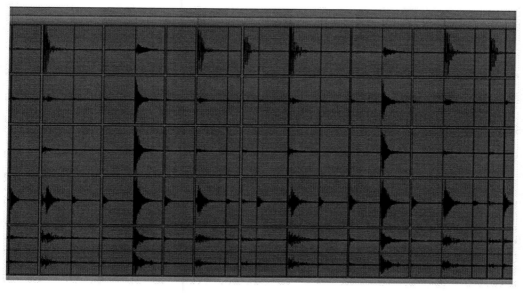

6 Click EDIT SMOOTHING to place Beat Detective into Edit Smoothing mode.

7 With the FILL GAPS & CROSSFADE option selected, choose a Crossfade Length of 5ms.

8 Click SMOOTH.

– Pro Tools will adjust each of the clip boundaries to remove any gaps that may have occurred while conforming and then perform crossfades on the boundaries.

Play the edited live drums into the Groove track:

1 Enable the "Kit" edit group.

2 Solo the drum tracks and the "Groove" track.

3 Listen for any clicks and pops and adjust fades as necessary.

4 Replace parts using material from other locations, as needed. Here you will replace parts that Beat Detective cannot fix:

- In bar 35, you may not have proper room to trim back to the previous hit. In this case, you can replace the problem area with the same material from bar 36.

- At 37|2|480, the hi-hat is considerably late relative to the kick drum. The kick drum is properly quantized, so moving the hat to the grid would make the kick early. Moving just the hi-hat clips would also be problematic, as phase coherency wont be maintained with other tracks. Once again, you can copy and paste a beat from elsewhere in the session.

5 When satisfied, Consolidate each drum track into a single clip:

- Select across each edited drum track.

- Choose Edit > Consolidate.

Consolidating will make it easier for Pro Tools to read the audio from disk, making errors much less likely in large sessions. Un-solo the drum tracks and listen to your changes in context.

Additional Beat Detective Considerations

- Beat Detective is a powerful and flexible tool. It takes practice and a strong familiarity with the material to be most effective. There is more than one way to use Beat Detective; experiment with what you have learned.

- The more straightforward the rhythm, the more bars you will be able to analyze at once. It may be necessary to select only a couple of bars at a time with complex material.

- Try Fill Gaps before using Fill and Crossfade during smoothing. If the result sounds good, you've saved time (crossfading can take a while) and kept the clips more organic in the process.

- Try Enhanced Resolution for Analyzing tracks. It may provide better results, depending on the material. Enhanced Resolution uses Pro Tools' state-of-the-art elastic audio algorithm.

Module 6 Key and Tempo

This module examines a variety of advanced techniques for editing and manipulating the tempo and key throughout a session.

Objectives:

- Insert and edit tempo changes and Bar|Beat Markers using Identify Beat

- Create Bar|Beat Markers using Beat Detective

- Understand the differences between tempo events and Bar|Beat Markers

- Use the Graphic Tempo Editor

- Use the Tempo Operations window

- Perform advanced, non-linear tempo changes over a selected range

- Add and edit Key Change events

Introduction

Pro Tools' tempo ruler and editor allow you to map and manipulate the tempo of a song in just about any way you can imagine. You can detect the tempo variations that exist in a recording and apply them to the tempo grid of the session, or create your own tempo events and apply them to MIDI and audio events. The Key ruler allows you to manipulate and conform MIDI performances within the bounds of any musical scale.

Tempo Basics

In Module 1, you learned how to set the song start point and derive a tempo from some recorded audio. You also reviewed how to set a default meter and insert meter changes.

Tempo Events

The simplest tempo edit you can make is to add a tempo change event somewhere in your song. When playback reaches this event, the tempo immediately changes to a new BPM value. In the Pro Tools 110 course, you learned how to add tempo events to the Tempo ruler and how to create more involved linear tempo changes using the Tempo Operations window. Both of these operations apply tick-based tempo events, meaning that each tempo event causes a specified tempo change to occur at a particular Bar|Beat location.

Bar|Beat Markers

By contrast, operations such as the Identify Beat command and Beat Detective's Bar|Beat Marker Generation establish tempo using sample-based events at fixed time locations, known as Bar|Beat Markers. The Bar|Beat Markers cause a specified beat or sub-beat to occur at a particular absolute time location. To make this work, Pro Tools calculates the necessary tempo for each range delineated by Bar|Beat Markers in your session.

In general, Tempo events are used to impose tempo on the song or performance, while Bar|Beat markers are used to align the tempo ruler to an existing performance.

Inserting and Editing Tempo Events

As you have learned in earlier courses, you can add a tempo event by doing one of the following:

- Click the ADD TEMPO CHANGE button at the left of the Tempo Ruler.

- CONTROL-CLICK (Mac) or START-CLICK (Windows) in the Tempo ruler (the cursor appears as a Grabber with a "+") at the location where you want to insert the event.

Either of these actions will open the Tempo Change window, where you can enter the Location and BPM value for the tempo change.

The new tempo event will be inserted at the specified location and will appear in the Tempo ruler. Tempo events appear as small green triangles followed by a note icon and a BPM notation.

To change the location of a tempo event do one of the following:

- Click and drag the triangle to a new location in the Tempo ruler.

- Double-click on the triangle and specify a new location in the Tempo Change window.

To change the BPM value of a tempo event:

- Double-click on the triangle and specify a new BPM value in the Tempo Change window.

Inserting and Editing Bar|Beat Markers

Bar|Beat Markers are created by the Identify Beat command or from Beat Detective's Bar|Beat Marker Generation operation. The Identify Beat command can be used simply to derive a global session tempo from an imported audio loop, as seen in Module 1, or to establish a detailed tempo map for a longer performance that was recorded without a click.

Typically, the Identify Beat command is used to calculate the tempo of a selection based on specified start and end Bar|Beat locations and a specified time signature. Bar|Beat Markers are inserted at the beginning and end of the selection, marking a range from which tempo is calculated.

You can also use the Identify Beat command to insert Bar|Beat Markers one at a time. In this case, tempo is calculated based on the range from the Session Start Marker or from a previous Bar|Beat Marker, if one exists.

To insert Bar|Beat Markers one at a time:

1 Place the Edit insertion point in your audio or MIDI clip at the location where you want to insert a Bar|Beat Marker.

2 Choose EVENT > IDENTIFY BEAT, or press COMMAND+I (Mac) or CTRL+I (Windows). The Add Bar|Beat Marker dialog box will open.

3 In the dialog box, specify the Bar|Beat location that corresponds to the selected point in the audio or MIDI performance.

4 If needed, specify the Time Signature to apply at the specified location.

5 Click OK to apply the change.

The new Bar|Beat Marker will be inserted at the specified location and will appear in the Tempo ruler. Bar|Beat Markers appear as small blue triangles; if other Bar|Beat Markers are present later in the session, the new marker will be followed by a note icon and a BPM notation.

 Bar\Beat Markers affect the tempo of the range they delineate. The new tempo takes effect beginning at the Song Start Marker or the previous Bar\Beat Marker, if present. If no Bar\Beat Marker exists after an inserted marker, the tempo will continue to the session end.

After inserting a Bar|Beat Marker, you can change its alignment relative to your sample-based audio to adjust or fine-tune its placement. You can also redefine the Bar|Beat location that a marker corresponds to, if needed.

To change the alignment of a Bar|Beat Marker:

• Click and drag the triangle to align it with a different point in a sample-based audio clip. The Tempo ruler will move with the Bar|Beat Marker, keeping the Bar|Beat location constant.

To redefine the bar and beat location of a Bar|Beat Marker:

• Double-click on the triangle and specify a new location in the Edit Bar|Beat Marker dialog box.

Tempo Events versus Bar | Beat Markers

Because tempo events are tick-based and Bar | Beat Markers are sample-based, they are logically incompatible and cannot be used simultaneously. The Tempo ruler can display either tempo events or Bar | Beat Markers at any given time, but not both together.

Changing the Tempo Ruler Display

If you add a Bar | Beat Marker to a session containing tempo events, the Tempo ruler will switch to Bar | Beat Marker display and all of the existing tempo events will be converted to Bar | Beat Markers. Similarly, if you add a tempo event to a session containing Bar | Beat Markers, the Tempo ruler will switch to Tempo Event display and all of the existing Bar | Beat Markers will be converted to tempo events.

You can also manually switch the Tempo ruler between displays, thereby converting all tempo events to Bar | Beat Markers, or vice versa.

To change the Tempo ruler display manually:

1   Press COMMAND (Mac) or CTRL (Windows) and click the ADD TEMPO CHANGE button.

2   Choose the desired display from the pop-up menu.

Tempo ruler pop-up menu

Tempo Event and Bar|Beat Marker Differences

Tempo events and Bar|Beat Markers both affect the tempo at specified points in your session, but they work in fundamentally different ways. The following chart provides a comparison:

Tempo Events...	Bar|Beat Markers...
Are tick-based	Are sample-based
Cause a specified tempo change to occur at the insertion point	Cause tempo to be calculated from neighboring Bar|Beat Markers based on the delimited range; do not cause a tempo change at the insertion point unless bordered by another Bar|Beat Marker to the right
Place the tempo change at a new bar and beat location when moved (dragged) in the Tempo ruler; retain BPM values after a move	Remain at the same the bar and beat location when moved (dragged) in the Tempo ruler; recalculate the BPM value of the marker to the immediate left after a move (recalculate their own BPM values if bordered by another Bar|Beat Marker to the right)
Cause neighboring MIDI events and audio clips on tick-based tracks to the right of the insertion point to shrink or expand to adjust for the new tempo	Cause neighboring MIDI events and audio clips on tick-based tracks on either side of the insertion point to shrink or expand to adjust for the new bar|beat position.

What is Affected by Tempo Events?

When you manipulate the tempo ruler, the changes affect existing material within tracks in different ways, depending on the track settings.

Sample-based tracks

Audio or MIDI/Instrument Tracks whose timebase is set to samples will be unaffected by tempo events. This includes Audio tracks with Elastic Audio plug-ins active.

Tick-based MIDI/Instrument Tracks

All clip start points and MIDI notes/events will be moved to conform to the tempo at each point in the session. MIDI note lengths will stretch or compress/MIDI performances will speed up or slow down to conform to the tempo.

Tick-based Audio Tracks – Without Elastic Audio

On Audio tracks whose timebase is set to ticks, but with no Elastic Audio plug-in, audio clips will move to maintain their start times relative to the Bar|Beat grid. The audio clips will maintain their original length (will not stretch or compress).

Tick-based Audio Tracks – With Elastic Audio

All audio clips will move to maintain their Bar|Beat position, and audio will be warped (stretched or compressed) to match the tempo ruler. Warp Markers will be created in Elastic Audio clips for every tempo event in the tempo ruler.

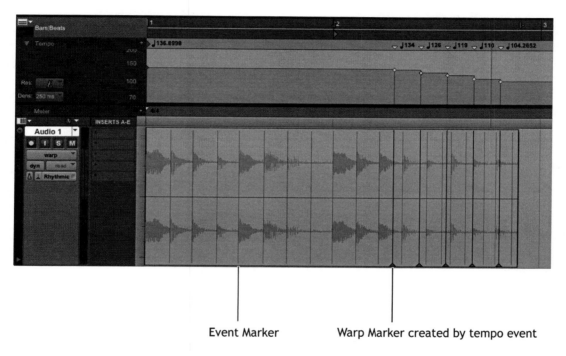

Event Marker   Warp Marker created by tempo event

Advanced Tempo Editing

In the following sections you will learn a number of advanced tools and techniques for manipulating the tempo ruler.

Graphic Tempo Editor

The Pro Tools tempo ruler can be expanded to display a graphical representation of your tempo changes using a menu command or the ruler's expand/collapse triangle.

Expand/Collapse triangle

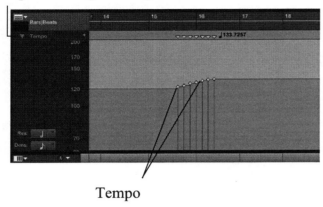

Tempo

Tempo Editor

To display the Tempo Editor do one of the following:

- Choose VIEW > RULERS > TEMPO EDITOR.
- Click the expand/collapse triangle on the Tempo ruler name plate.

The Tempo Editor is displayed in a resizable window beneath the Tempo ruler and can be used to view and edit tempo information graphically.

Editing Tempo Events in the Tempo Editor

Tempo events in the Tempo Editor can be edited using any of the following methods:

- Individual tempo events can be dragged horizontally and vertically with the Grabber tool to adjust their locations and bpm values.
- New tempo events can be drawn individually or as a continuous series using the Pencil tool.
- A group of selected tempo events can be scaled up or down with the Trim tool.
- Tempo events can be copied, pasted, nudged, and shifted.

Using the Grabber Tool

The Grabber tool lets you change tempo settings by dragging individual tempo events in the Tempo Editor.

To edit a tempo event with the Grabber tool do one of the following:

- Drag the vertical tempo line to the left or right to adjust the location of the tempo event.

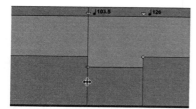

Moving a tempo line with the Grabber tool

- Drag the tempo event handle up or down to increase or decrease tempo.

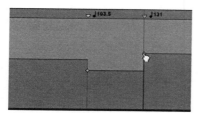

Moving a tempo event handle

To remove a tempo event with the Grabber tool:

- OPTION-CLICK (Mac) or ALT-CLICK (Windows) on a tempo event handle with the Grabber tool to erase it.

Using the Pencil Tool

Tempo events can be drawn in the Tempo Editor using the Pencil tool, with the following shapes:

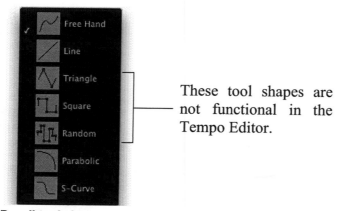

These tool shapes are not functional in the Tempo Editor.

Pencil tool shape pop-up menu

The shape you draw is reproduced as a series of steps according to the Tempo Edit Density setting.

Selecting Edit Density

The Tempo Edit Density button in the Tempo Editor lets you specify the density of tempo events created in the Tempo Ruler when you draw a tempo curve with the Pencil tool.

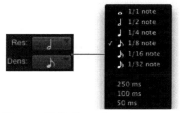

Tempo Edit Density pop-up menu

Selecting Resolution

The Tempo Resolution pop-up menu in the Tempo Editor lets you specify the note value that BPM rates are based on when you draw a tempo curve with the Pencil tool. In most cases, the simplest option is to choose FOLLOW METRONOME CLICK. This will use the beat lengths referenced by the current meter, i.e. if the current meter is 4/4, the bpm will reference quarter-note beats; 6/8 sections will reference eighth notes, etc.

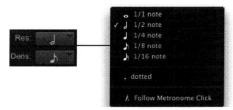

Tempo Resolution pop-up menu

Curve Adjustment Mode

Immediately after you draw new tempos using the Pencil tool, a tempo curve appears in blue, outlining the newly created tempo graph. Blue adjustment handles also appear on the curve, which you can use to adjust the shape and size of the new tempo graph.

Tempo Curve Adjustment Handles

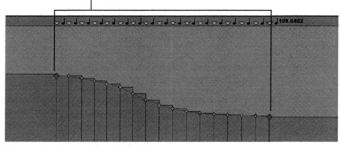

Tempo curve adjustment

All tempo events under the curve will change as you move the Tempo Curve Adjustment Handles. To suspend changes while you adjust the curve shape, press CONTROL *(Mac) or* START *(Windows) while dragging the adjustment handles. Tempo events will change to fit the curve when you release the mouse.*

The blue adjustment handles are active only until you select a new tool or execute a new command.

Using the Trim Tool

The Trim tool lets you scale all the tempo events in your session or scale selected tempo events only. The Trim tool also lets you stretch a selection of tempo events to cover a longer or shorter area in the timeline.

To scale tempo events with the Trim tool:

1 Open the Tempo Editor.

2 Using the SELECTOR tool, select the range of tempo events that you wish to affect (or select nothing if you want to scale all events in the session).

3 Select the TRIM tool.

4 Then do one of the following:

– To scale the tempo of the selected events, click within the selected area and drag up or down.

Changing selected tempos with the Trim tool

– To create a linear speed up or slow down across the existing events, click either the start or end handle for the selected range, and drag up or down.

Adjusting the amount of tempo change with the Trim tool

- To move the tempo events closer together or further apart in time, click the selection boundary on either side of the selected range and drag horizontally. Tempo events will maintain their relative spacing to each other but will be stretched or compacted to extend across a larger or smaller time span.

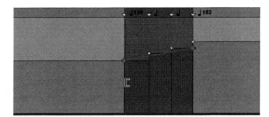

Changing the rate of tempo change with the Trim tool

Selecting Tempo Events

You can easily select a single tempo event, or an entire tempo curve within the Tempo Editor.

To select a tempo event in the Tempo Editor do one of the following:

- Using the SELECTOR or GRABBER tool, double-click anywhere between the vertical tempo lines. The range between tempo events will be selected, along with the left-most tempo event, delineating the start of the range.

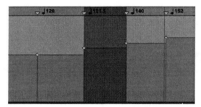

Selecting a single tempo event

- Using the SELECTOR or GRABBER tool, make a selection that extends across the desired vertical tempo event line.

To select a tempo curve in the Tempo Editor:

- Using the SELECTOR or GRABBER tool, triple-click between the vertical tempo lines anywhere in the curve that you wish to select.

Moving, Cutting, Pasting, and Nudging in the Tempo Editor

Tempo events within a selected range can be moved, rearranged, and removed using the same techniques you would use for editing audio.

To move a selected range of tempo events in the Tempo Editor do one of the following:

- With the GRABBER tool, click on the vertical tempo line or tempo event handle of any selected tempo event and drag horizontally. All tempo events within the selection will move as a group.

- Use the CUT, COPY and PASTE commands as you would with track data.

- Use the Nudge keys ([+] and [–]) on the keypad to move the selected events by the current nudge amount.

Changing the Linearity Display Mode

You can choose to view the Edit window in either a Linear Tick (Bars | Beats) scale or a Linear Sample (absolute) Time Scale. MIDI and Instrument Tracks, audio tracks, and tempo curves can appear and function very differently depending on the timebase display settings you choose.

To change the timebase display:

1   Click on the LINEARITY DISPLAY MODE SELECTOR in the Edit window toolbar.

2   Select the desired timebase from the LINEARITY DISPLAY MODE POP-UP menu.

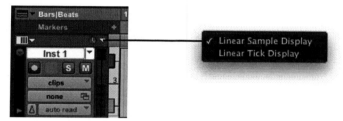

Linearity Display Mode pop-up menu

Understanding the Display Modes

Linear Sample Display Mode is Pro Tools' default display mode. In this mode, tempo changes affect the display of tick-based tracks—when the tempo increases, tick-based material compacts on screen providing a visual indication that the material will play back faster; when tempo decreases, the same material stretches out on screen, indicating that it will play back more slowly. Tempo changes do not affect the display of sample-based tracks and waveforms in this mode.

In Linear Sample Display Mode, the Edit window scroll speed or playback cursor speed remains constant during playback and recording and is not affected by the session tempo or tempo changes.

Linear Tick Display Mode is an alternate mode that keeps the display of tick-based tracks constant, so that the length of each measure is displayed consistently regardless of tempo. In this mode, tempo changes affect the display of sample-based tracks and waveforms—when the tempo increases, sample-based material expands on screen providing a visual indication that it will extend across more measures; when tempo decreases, the same material shrinks on screen, indicating that it will extend across fewer measures.

In Linear Tick Display Mode, the Edit window scroll speed or playback cursor speed changes during playback and recording, based on the session tempo and tempo changes. In this mode, Pro Tools playback visually "speeds up" and "slows down" according to the tempo.

Using the Display Modes with the Tempo Editor

The Linearity Display Mode also determines whether the Tempo Editor displays and creates tempo events in a Bars|Beats or Absolute timebase.

When using Linear Sample Display Mode, the display of tempo events is sample-based and their bar and beat locations can shift after a tempo curve is drawn.

When using Linear Tick Display Mode, the tempo events are tick-based and their Bar|Beat locations remain constant after a tempo curve is drawn—though their relation to audio is scaled, resulting in a new sample locations.

 Drawing tempo events using Linear Sample Display Mode can cause Bar|Beat-based material to move in non-intuitive ways. Avid recommends using Linear Tick Display when drawing tempo changes.

Tempo Operations Window

The Tempo Operations window (Event > Tempo Operations > Tempo Operations Window) lets you define or manipulate tempo events over a range of time (or measures). The time range is specified in the time format chosen for your Main Time Scale. In addition, the Tempo Operations window lets you do the following:

- Fit a specific number of Bars|Beats into a precise time range.
- Create tempos that speed up or slow down, both linearly and non-linearly along various curves.
- Scale and stretch existing tempos by a percentage amount.

The Tempo Operations window has six pages, selectable from the pop-up menu at the top of the window. The pages correspond to each of the six types of tempo operations that Pro Tools provides. The Tempo Operations pages include the following:

- Constant—This page lets you create a constant tempo over a selected range of time.
- Linear—This page lets you create tempo events that change evenly over a selected range of time.
- Parabolic—This page lets you create tempo events that speed up or slow down following a parabolic curve.
- S-Curve—This page lets you create tempo events that speed up or slow down following an S-curve.
- Scale—This page lets you scale tempos within the selection by a percentage amount.
- Stretch—This page lets you select a range of tempo events and apply them to a larger or smaller selection area.

Common Controls

Each Tempo Operations page has a number of controls for configuring how it operates. The following basic controls are common to all Tempo Operations pages:

- Advanced Checkbox—When the Advanced checkbox is selected, the selection range changes to the Main Time Scale format, and additional advanced options become available.

- Selection Start and End Fields—These fields are used to specify the start and end points for the tempo change in Bars|Beats (or in the Main Time Scale when using Advanced mode). When an Edit selection is made, the Start and End fields will automatically fill in with the selection boundaries. Likewise, changing a value in one of these fields will update the Edit selection range accordingly.

- Preserve Tempo after Selection checkbox—When this checkbox is selected, the original tempo setting is preserved at the selection end point after the tempo operation. When unselected, the last tempo event created by the tempo operation continues to the end of the session or until the next tempo event in the session.

The advanced controls on each page offer additional configuration options. These controls only display when the Advanced checkbox is selected. Common advanced controls include the following:

- Calculate—This pop-up menu lets you select a parameter to automatically calculate based on the other values entered. The field for the selected parameter becomes deactivated.

- Resolution—This option lets you choose the BPM note value for your tempo setting.

 Selecting FOLLOW METRONOME CLICK *sets the tempo BPM note value to mirror the click value set in the meter markers.*

- Density—This option lets you specify the density of the tempo change events written to the Tempo ruler.

Common controls, basic   Common controls, advanced

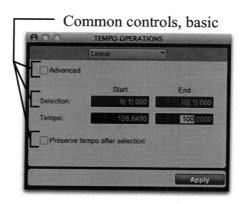
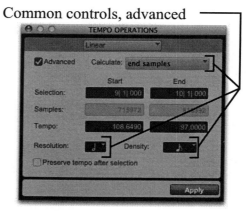

Common controls displayed on the Linear Tempo Operations page

Additional controls are available on each page, providing configuration options specific to that page's function.

Constant Page

You can use the Constant page to create a constant tempo over a selected range of time.

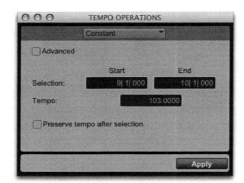

Constant page of the Tempo Operations window

The options provided on the Constant page include the following:

- Tempo—Use this field to specify the tempo to apply to the selected range. This field grays out when Calculate (advanced option) is set to tempo.

- Calculate (Advanced)—This pop-up menu lets you choose to calculate either the tempo or the operation End Time.

- Resolution (Advanced)—See above.

- Density (Advanced)—See above.

- End Time (Advanced)—Use this field when the Calculate option is set to tempo to specify the end time for the operation. Changing this field will cause the Tempo field to recalculate accordingly.

 When the Main Time Scale is set to Bars|Beats, the operation End Time is displayed in the Sub Time Scale; otherwise, it is displayed in Bars|Beats.

Linear Page

As you learned in the Pro Tools 110 course, you can use the Linear page to create tempos that change evenly over a selected range of time.

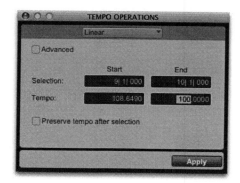

Linear page of the Tempo Operations window

The options provided in the Linear page are similar to those in the Constant page, with the exception that the Tempo parameters allow you to specify different start and end tempos.

 For additional details on the Linear page options, see the Pro Tools 110 book.

Parabolic Page

You can use the Parabolic page to create tempos that accelerate or decelerate, following a tempo curve that changes the tempo more rapidly or less rapidly over the selection time.

Parabolic page of the Tempo Operations window

The options provided on the Parabolic page include the following:

- Tempo Start and End—Use these fields to specify the start and end tempos for the tempo change range.

- Curvature—Use the Curvature field or slider to specify the tempo curve, as displayed in the graph area. Negative numbers create a tempo curve that has more rapid tempo change at the beginning of the time range; positive numbers create a tempo curve that has more rapid tempo change at the end of the time range.

- Calculate (Advanced)—This pop-up menu lets you choose to calculate the operation End Time, the start tempo, the end tempo, or the curvature.

- Resolution (Advanced)—See above.

- Density (Advanced)—See above.

- End Time (Advanced)—Use this field to specify the end time for the operation. Changing this field will cause the selected Calculate field to recalculate accordingly. This field grays out when the Calculate option is set to the operation End Time.

S-Curve Page

You can use the S-Curve page to create tempos that accelerate or decelerate, following a tempo curve with a definable breakpoint that determines mid-curve times and tempo values.

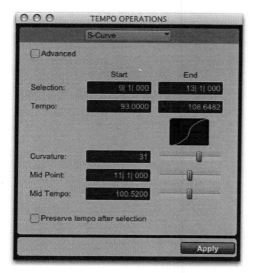

S-Curve page of the Tempo Operations window

The options provided on the S-Curve page include the following:

- Tempo Start and End—Use these fields to specify the start and end tempos for the tempo change range.

- Curvature—Use the Curvature field or slider to specify the tempo curve, as displayed in the graph area. Negative numbers create a curve that changes rapidly at the start and end of the of the range, and slowly through the middle; positive numbers create a curve that changes slowly near the start and end, and quickly through the middle.

- Mid Point—Use the Mid Point field or slider to specify the Bar|Beat location for the curve midpoint.

- Mid Tempo—Use the Mid Tempo field or slider to specify the tempo at the midpoint.

- Calculate (Advanced)—This pop-up menu lets you choose to calculate the curve Midpoint, the operation End Time, the start tempo, the mid tempo, or the end tempo.

- Resolution (Advanced)—See above.

- Density (Advanced)—See above.

- End Time (Advanced)—Use this field to specify the end time for the operation. Changing this field will cause the selected Calculate field to recalculate accordingly. This field grays out when the Calculate option is set to the operation End Time.

Scale Page

You can use the Scale page to scale tempos within a selection by a percentage amount.

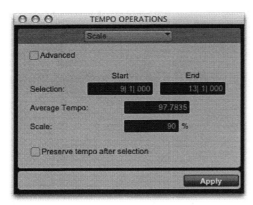

Scale page of the Tempo Operations window

The options provided on the Scale page include the following:

- Average Tempo—This field will display the average tempo, in BPM, for the selected range. Changing the tempo value will cause the Scale percentage to update accordingly.

- Scale—This field specifies the percentage change to apply to the selected tempo events. Changing the Scale percentage will cause the Average Tempo value to change accordingly.

- Calculate (Advanced)—This pop-up menu lets you choose to calculate either the operation End Time or the tempo.

- Scale (Advanced)—This pop-up menu lets you choose to scale all tempos, the start tempo, or the end tempo.

- End Time (Advanced)—Use this field to specify the end time for the operation. Changing this field will cause the tempo to calculate accordingly. This field grays out when the Calculate option is set to the operation End Time.

Stretch Page

You can use the Stretch page to select a range of tempo events and apply them to a larger or smaller selection area.

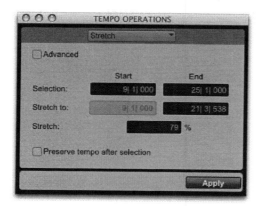

Stretch page of the Tempo Operations window

The options provided on the Stretch page include the following:

- Stretch To End—Use this field to specify a new end point for the selected tempo events. Changing the end point will cause the Stretch percentage to recalculate accordingly.

- Stretch—Use this field to specify the percentage change to apply to the timing of the selected tempo events. Increasing the Stretch percentage will spread the tempo events out across a larger selection; decreasing the Stretch percentage will compress the tempo events into a shorter selection. Changing this value will cause the Stretch to End value to recalculate accordingly.

- Stretch pop-up menu (Advanced)—This pop-up menu lets you choose to adjust either the selection end point or the selection start point to accommodate the new range as determined by the Stretch percentage.

Working with Key Changes

Like the Tempo and Meter rulers, the Key Signature ruler can be used to store events on the timeline—in this case, the ruler events represent key signatures and key changes. Key signatures can be used for certain functions that can be applied to MIDI or Instrument Tracks, such as transposing diatonically in key or constraining pitches to a key.

Adding, Editing, and Deleting Key Signatures

The default key signature when you open a new Pro Tools session is C major. You can add, edit, or delete key signatures using methods similar to those for adding, editing, or deleting events on other rulers.

To add a key signature:

1 Do one of the following:

   – Choose EVENT > ADD KEY CHANGE.

   – Click the ADD KEY SIGNATURE button ("+" symbol) at the left of the Key Signature ruler.

   – Press the CONTROL key (Mac) or the START key (Windows) and click in the Key Signature ruler where you want to insert the Key Change event.

   The Key Change dialog box will open.

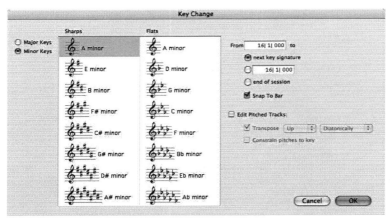

Key Change dialog box

2 Select the desired mode (major or minor) and the desired key in the dialog box.

3 Specify start and end details as desired:

   – Set the starting point and duration for the new key using the FROM field and the TO options.

   – To constrain the resulting Key Change events to a bar-based grid, select the SNAP TO BAR checkbox. Any new Key Change events that are added will be quantized to the nearest bar.

You can also set the duration for a key change by making a selection in the Edit window prior to adding the key change. This will fill in the From and To fields automatically based on the selection boundaries.

4   Specify how the key change will affect existing MIDI notes on Pitched tracks as follows:

   – If desired, select EDIT PITCHED TRACKS to transpose existing MIDI data on pitched MIDI or Instrument Tracks. When this option is selected, the TRANSPOSE and CONSTRAIN options become enabled.

 If you select EDIT PITCHED TRACKS but do not select a TRANSPOSE or CONSTRAIN option, no change will be applied to existing MIDI data.

   – To transpose notes up or down, select the TRANSPOSE option and the transpose direction and choose whether to transpose diatonically or chromatically.

 The choice of diatonic vx. chromatic transposition only affects key changes between modes (major to minor or vice versa).

   – To constrain pitches to the notes in the new key, select CONSTRAIN PITCHES TO KEY. With this option selected, individual notes will be transposed to the nearest diatonic pitch in the new key, whether the overall performance is transposed or not.

5   Click OK to apply the key change and close the dialog box.

To edit an existing key change event:

1   With any Edit tool selected, double-click on a Key Change event on the Key Signature ruler. The Key Change dialog box will open.

2   Select the appropriate key change options as described above.

3   Click OK to apply the key change and close the dialog box.

To delete an existing key change event:

1   With any Edit tool selected, OPTION-CLICK (Mac) or ALT-CLICK (Windows) on a Key Change event on the Key Signature ruler. The Remove Key Signature dialog box will open, allowing you to specify options for editing pitched tracks.

2   Select the appropriate options for transposing notes relative to the previous key signature in the session and click OK.

3   The event will be deleted from the ruler, and the notes on any pitched MIDI or Instrument tracks will transpose according to the selected options.

Tips for Using Key Signatures

Following are some rules of thumb that apply to key signatures and key changes on tracks with existing MIDI data:

- Pro Tools interprets the pitch of existing MIDI data in relation to the key signature currently in effect at any given point on the timeline. If no key changes have been added, all MIDI notes are interpreted as diatonic or chromatic relative to the default key of C major.

- In order for Pro Tools to transpose existing MIDI data correctly, you need to first identify the correct base key. To do this, determine the key of the existing MIDI data on pitched tracks and insert the corresponding Key Change event on the Key Signatures ruler. DO NOT enable EDIT PITCHED TRACKS with this Key Change event.

- MIDI or Instrument Tracks that are used for drum machines, samplers, or other devices that rely on specific key mappings should be changed to non-pitched tracks prior to adding Key Change events that transpose or conform MIDI pitches. You do not want data on these tracks to be affected by key changes.

 To change a track to non-pitched, click the track's Playlist selector and deselect the PITCHED *option.*

Deselect the Pitched option for drum tracks.

- To revert to a previous key after inserting a Key Change event and transposing pitched tracks, do one of the following:
    - Undo the key change, if possible.
    - Delete the Key Change event, select Edit Pitched Tracks, and transpose the Pitched tracks in the proper direction to match the original pitch.

Example

Suppose you have three Instrument Tracks in your session. The first two tracks contain guitar and bass parts, respectively, which are played back via an Xpand! plug-in on each track. The third track triggers drum patterns played by the Strike plug-in. Let's say the guitar and bass parts were originally recorded in the key of C minor and you would like to modulate to D minor for the final chorus. To accomplish this, you would do the following:

1 Insert a Key Change event at the beginning of the session (1|1|000), identifying the key as C minor.

2 Deselect the Pitched option in the track Playlist selector for the drum track.

3 Insert a Key Change event at the final chorus, changing the key to D minor and enabling the options for EDIT PITCHED TRACKS and TRANSPOSE UP DIATONICALLY. The MIDI data on the guitar and bass tracks will transpose up a full step to D minor. The MIDI data on the drum track will remain unchanged.

Review Questions

1   Can the Tempo ruler display tempo events and Bar|Beat Markers simultaneously? Explain. (See "Tempo Events versus Bar|Beat Markers" on page 169.)

2   What happens to existing tempo events when you change the Tempo ruler display to Bar|Beat Markers? (See "Changing the Tempo Ruler Display" on page 169.)

3   Describe the differences in the ways tempo events and Bar|Beat Markers affect tempo. (See "Tempo Event and Bar|Beat Marker Differences" on page 170.)

4   What is the Graphic Tempo Editor and when would you use it? (See "Graphic Tempo Editor" on page 172.)

5   Describe two different methods to display the Graphic Tempo Editor. (See "Graphic Tempo Editor" on page 172.)

6   What Pencil shapes can you use to edit tempo? Which shapes are unavailable for editing tempo? (See "Using the Pencil Tool" on page 173.)

7   Describe three ways to use the Trim tool to adjust a range of tempo events in the Tempo Editor. (See "Using the Trim Tool" on page 175.)

8   What is the difference between Linear Sample Display mode and Linear Tick Display mode? How does the display mode affect Pro Tools' scroll speed during playback? (See "Changing the Linearity Display Mode" on page 177.)

9   What function does the Advanced checkbox have in the Tempo Operations window? What function does the Calculate pop-up menu offer? (See "Tempo Operations Window" on page 178.)

10   What types of tracks are NOT affected by key change events? (See "Working with Key Changes" on page 186.)

Module 7 Arranging and Producing

This module covers larger scale editing techniques used when arranging a composition.

Objectives:
- Use Window Configurations
- Automatically replace clips in the timeline
- Replace recorded sounds with samples using Sound Replacer
- Use Playlists
- Arrange songs with Cut and Insert Time
- Copy, Paste, and Duplicate entire sections of your song.
- Use Clip Groups for song arrangement

Introduction

Module 5 was concerned with editing the contents of performances, clips, and loops. In this module you will take a step back from the details, and consider the Pro Tools features that aid in broader song-level editing and arrangement.

Window Configurations

To start this chapter, let's look at a powerful house-keeping tool that can dramatically speed up your work: Window Configurations. Window Configurations provide a means of managing the display of the windows in your session, as well as the display settings for the Edit, Mix, Transport, MIDI Editor, and Score Editor windows.

A window configuration can store the location and size of all Pro Tools' windows and floating windows (apart from the Window Configuration List itself). Pro Tools lets you store up to 99 Window Configurations with your session.

Note: You can use Import Session Data to import Window Configurations from another session into your current session.

Window Configuration List

The Window Configuration List lets you create, recall, and manage Window Configurations. The Window Configuration List operates much like the Memory Locations window.

To open the Window Configuration List:

- Select WINDOW > CONFIGURATIONS > WINDOW CONFIGURATION LIST. The Window Configuration List will display in a floating window.

Tip: Press COMMAND+OPTION+J (Mac) or CTRL+ALT+J (Windows) to show or hide the Window Configuration List.

The Window Configuration List. The active configuration is highlighted.

To create a new Window Configuration:

1 Open the windows you want to include in the new Window Configuration; configure the size, position, and display settings for the windows as you want them on screen.

2 Do one of the following:

   – Choose WINDOW > CONFIGURATIONS > NEW CONFIGURATION.

   – Choose NEW CONFIGURATION from the pop-up menu in the Window Configuration List.

   The NEW WINDOW CONFIGURATION dialog box will appear.

Note: On the numeric keypad, type Period (.), a number (1–99), and then Plus (+) to add a new Window Configuration at that number slot. If a Window Configuration already exists at that numbered slot, the new Window Configuration overwrites it.

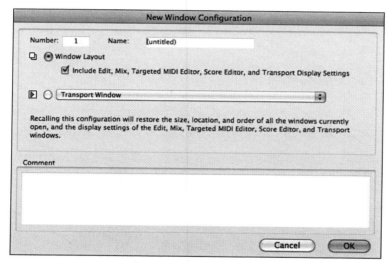

3 Do one of the following:

   – Select WINDOW LAYOUT and choose whether to include Edit, Mix, Targeted MIDI Editor, Score Editor, and Transport display settings.

   – From the DISPLAY SETTINGS pop-up menu, choose a specific window as the Window Configuration target.

4 Name the Window Configuration and enter any applicable comments.

5 Click OK to save the settings.

Settings Included in Window Configurations

Window Configurations store different settings, depending on the options selected when creating them. The available options and their functions are as follows:

- Window Layout radio button—Choosing Window Layout stores a snapshot of all windows that are open, their locations, and their sizes.

- Include Edit, Mix, Targeted MIDI Editor, Score Editor, and Transport Display Settings checkbox—When this box is checked (and Window Layout is selected), all display settings for all main windows are stored. (Display settings for each window are described below.)

- Display Settings pop-up menu—Choosing an option in this menu stores all display settings for the selected window, as described below. This option does not store window locations or sizes.

  - Edit Window Display Settings—This option stores the following display settings:

    Width/height/display status of the Tracks List and Groups List

    Ruler Views (rulers currently displayed)

    Column displays (Inserts, Comments, etc.)

    Tempo Editor display

    Display status of the Transport controls (shown/hidden in Edit window toolbar)

  - Mix Window Display Settings—This option stores the following display settings:

    Width/height/display status of the Tracks List and Groups List

    Track row displays (Inserts, Sends, instruments, etc.)

    Narrow Mix display (active/inactive)

  - Transport Window Display Settings—This option stores the following display settings:

    Counters display

    MIDI Controls display

    Expanded view display

View Filter Icons

Like the Memory Locations window, the Window Configuration List has icons indicating the types of settings that are included in each stored configuration. The icons in the menu bar act as show/hide filters for your Window Configurations. Clicking any of these icons greys it out and hides the Window Configurations that matched only that icon (i.e., they don't match any of the remaining icons).

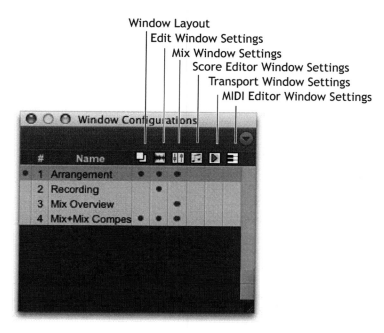

Recalling Window Configurations

Like memory locations, Window Configurations can be recalled in two ways.

To recall a Window Configuration, do one of the following:

- In the Window Configuration List, click a Window Configuration to recall it.

- On the numeric keypad, press Period (.) followed by the number of the Window Configuration (1–99), and then Asterisk (*).

Updating Window Configurations

After you recall a stored Window Configuration, you can make changes to the window layout and window settings, and then update the stored Window Configuration with your changes. You can do this manually, or you can have Pro Tools automatically update the active configuration.

To manually update a Window Configuration, do one of the following:

- Choose WINDOW > CONFIGURATIONS > UPDATE "CONFIGURATION NAME".

- The active Window Configuration will update to include any changes to its stored properties (Window Layout and Window Display Settings, if included).

- From the Window Configuration List pop-up menu, choose UPDATE "CONFIGURATION NAME". The selected Window Configuration will update with any changes to its stored properties.

To have Pro Tools automatically update the active Window Configuration, do one of the following:

- Select WINDOW > CONFIGURATIONS > AUTO-UPDATE ACTIVE CONFIGURATION.

- From the Window Configuration List pop-up menu, select AUTO-UPDATE ACTIVE CONFIGURATION.

When Auto-Update Active Configuration is selected, the active Window Configuration will update with every change to the Window Layout and Window Display Settings. This enables you to create a Window Configuration that tracks ad hoc changes and allows you to return to those settings after invoking a different Window Configuration.

Storing Window Configurations in Memory Locations

You can store a Window Configuration in any memory location. This is a very powerful way to store and recall a large number of display preferences. For example, you can recall Window Layout, Edit and Mix Window settings, zoom settings, track show/hide settings, and track heights with one click.

To store a Window Configuration in a memory location:

1 Create one or more Window Configurations as described above.

2 Create a new memory location, or open an existing one by double-clicking on it in the Memory Locations window. The NEW MEMORY LOCATION or EDIT MEMORY LOCATION dialog box will open.

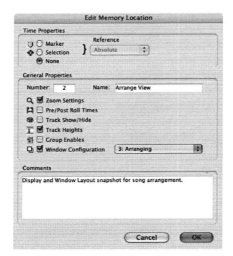

3   In the dialog box, select the Window Configuration option, and choose a configuration from the pop-up list. Select any other desired options.

4   Click OK to save the settings.

Recalling this memory location will also recall the selected Window Configuration.

Replacing Clips

A common production decision is to improve a track by swapping out certain loops or drum sounds. This section describes two different techniques for doing this. The Replace Clip command is a built-in Pro Tools feature that allows you to quickly swap out one clip (or multiple instances of the clip) with another. Sound Replacer is an Audiosuite plug-in that can intelligently replace drum sounds within audio clips.

The Replace Clip Command

On Pro Tools HD systems, the built-in Replace Clip command is a quick way to replace one clip with another, or to replace all the occurrences of a clip in your session.

Pro Tools provides two different ways to access the Replace Clip functionality: via drag-and-drop, or via the Replace Clip command in the Clip List pop-up menu.

To replace clips using Drag-and-Drop:

- Press COMMAND+SHIFT (Mac) or CTRL+SHIFT (Windows) and drag the replacement clip from the Clip List onto the clip you wish to replace in a track. (The clip in the track should not be selected.) The the target clip in the track will be outlined as you mouse over it.

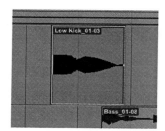

Target clip to be replaced

To replace clips using the Replace Clip command:

1   Select the clip to replace in a track.

2   Right-click on the replacement clip in the Clip List and choose REPLACE CLIP from the contextual menu.

Replace Clip command

Whichever method you use, the Replace Clip dialog will appear:

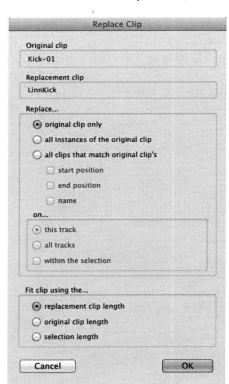

Replace Clip dialog box

The Replace Clip dialog box has several sections, which provide the following options:

- REPLACE section:
  - Original Clip Only: Replaces the targeted clip only, using the replacement clip dragged from the Clip List.
  - All Instances of the Original Clip: Replaces all instances of the targeted clip in the track, session, or selection, based on the criteria selected in the next section.
  - All Clips that Math Original Clip's start position/end position/name: Replaces all clips within the track, session, or selection, based on the criteria below.
- ON section:
  - This track/all tracks/within the selection: Further defines which instances of the clip are replaced, including the option to replace within a selection.
- FIT CLIP USING section:
  - Replacement clip legnth: The replacement clip is placed in its entirety, regardless of the length of the target clip.
  - Original clip legnth: The replacement clip replaces the original and is trimmed to match the original length, if needed.
  - Selection legnth: If a playlist selection extends beyond the target clip, the replacement clip is trimmed to the selection length, if needed.

Using SoundReplacer

SoundReplacer is an AudioSuite plug-in that replaces individual hits within audio tracks (especially drum or percussion tracks) with different sound samples. For example, you can replace your recorded snare drum with a more suitable sample (or samples) from your sound library.

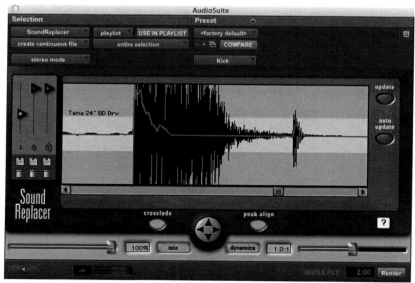

SoundReplacer plug-in window

SoundReplacer Overview

SoundReplacer detects transients in an audio recording, and marks them according to three separate trigger thresholds (amplitudes). These hits can then be replaced with samples of your choosing. Variations in amplitude within the performance determine which sample is triggered at each detected transient. For example, you could assign a soft snare hit to a low trigger threshold, a standard snare to a medium trigger threshold, and a rim shot snare to trigger only at the highest trigger threshold.

As another example, you could use SoundReplacer to manipulate a loop comprised of two or three different drums (e.g., kick, snare, hat). SoundReplacer could replace one or more of the elements of the loop based on their different amplitudes.

As it replaces sounds, SoundReplacer matches the levels of the original hits when it places the new samples, preserving the original dynamics of the performance.

Replacement audio events can be written to a new audio track or mixed and re-written to the source audio track.

To get started with SoundReplacer, do the following:

1   Choose AudioSuite > Other > SoundReplacer. The SoundReplacer plug-in will open.

2   Make a selection on a track that contains audio you wish to replace.

3   Click Update on the right side of the plug-in. The waveform display will update to show the selected audio.

Waveform Display

The SoundReplacer waveform display shows the audio that you have selected for replacement.

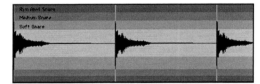

Waveform display with trigger markers shown

The Zoomer button in the SoundReplacer plug-in window (bottom center) allows you to increase or decrease the magnification in the waveform display.

If you change the audio selection on the source track, you can click Update to update the waveform display. If you select Auto Update, SoundReplacer will automatically update the waveform display each time you make a new selection or begin playback.

Trigger Threshold

The Trigger Threshold sliders set the levels for triggering the three replacement audio files.

Threshold controls

The Trigger Threshold sliders are color-coded and correspond to the three amplitude zones for triggering replacement samples. The controls under each Threshold slider allow you to load and unload replacement samples.

To load replacement samples, do the following:

1   Click on the floppy disk icon beneath a slider.

2   Navigate to the drive location where the desired file is located.

3   Select the file and click CHOOSE. The sample will be loaded into the corresponding amplitude zone.

To unload samples, do the following:

• Click on the trash can icon beneath a slider. The sample will be unloaded and the corresponding amplitude zone will be empty.

Load/Unload Sound Icons

To audition a replacement sample before loading it into SoundReplacer, use the Import Audio command in Pro Tools. Alternatively, you can also use the Workspace browser to quickly audition samples. Once you have located and previewed the desired audio files, you can then load them into SoundReplacer using the Load Sound icons.

 SoundReplacer can only load Whole-File Clips. To use a Clip as a replacement sample, you must first save it as a Whole-File Clip.

Once replacement samples are loaded, you can drag the Threshold sliders to the desired amplitude levels. Color-coded trigger markers will appear in the Waveform at points where the source audio signal triggers the sample for that amplitude zone. The color of each Trigger marker corresponds to the matching Threshold slider. This allows you to see, at a glance, which replacement samples will be triggered and where.

Crossfade

When Crossfade is selected, SoundReplacer crossfades between replacement audio files in different amplitude zones. This helps smooth the transition between them.

When Crossfade is deselected, SoundReplacer hard switches between replacement audio files in different amplitude zones.

Crossfading is particularly useful for adding a sense of realism to drum replacement. Crossfading between a straight snare hit and a rim shot, for example, results in a much more "live" feel than simply hard switching between the two samples. However, if you are using Sound Replacer to replace different types of drums, such as in a mixed loop, you'll want to disable crossfading.

Peak Align

When Peak Align is on, SoundReplacer aligns the peak of the replacement file with the peak of the source file in a way that best maintains phase coherency. When Peak Align is off, SoundReplacer aligns the beginning of the replacement file with the trigger threshold point. Depending on the characteristics of your source and replacement audio files, using Peak Align can significantly affect the timing of audio events in the replacement file. It is essential that you choose the option most appropriate to the material that you are replacing.

Mix

The Mix slider adjusts the mix of the replacement audio file with the original source file. Higher percentage values weight the mix toward the replacement audio. Lower percentage values weight the mix toward the original source audio.

 Setting Mix to 50% and clicking PREVIEW *allows you to audition source audio and replacement audio together to check the accuracy of replacement sample timing.*

Dynamics

The Dynamics slider controls how closely the audio events in the replacement file track the dynamics of the source file:

- Setting the ratio to 1.00 matches the dynamics of the source file.

- Increasing the ratio above 1.00 expands the dynamic range so that softer hits are softer, and louder hits are louder. This is useful if the source material lacks variation in its dynamic range.

- Decreasing the ratio below 1.00 compresses the dynamic range so that there is less variation between loud and soft hits. This is useful if the dynamics of the source material are too extreme.

The Dynamics button provides a quick means of switching off amplitude tracking.

TL Drum Rehab

TL Drum Rehab plug-in window

Another plug-in that performs a similar task to Sound Replacer is TL Drum Rehab. Drum Rehab is a Native plug-in, working in real time on a track, instead of processing a selection offline.

Playlist Editing

You encountered the concept of Playlists in Module 2, where they were used to store and compile multiple recording takes within a single track. Here, we will explore Pro Tools' powerful Playlist functionality fully, and see how it can be used to try out and audition different edits and arrangements.

In Pro Tools, any sequence of data of the same type in a track is referred to as a playlist. Each playlist is as long as the session, i.e. a playlist is not a sub-section of a track's data. For example, a newly created Audio track has one audio playlist—also called an edit playlist—into which audio clips can be placed or recorded. However, extra edit playlists can be added to an Audio track, and each can contain entirely different sequences of clips on them. You can switch between these playlists in the track, with one being active at any time.

MIDI, Instrument, and Video tracks can also have multiple playlists. The graphs representing automation data for each track/plug-in parameter are also called playlists, but each track can only contain one automation playlist for each parameter.

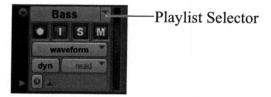

Playlist Selector

Playlists can be one of your most valuable tools as a producer, because they let you try out different ideas and arrangements without losing existing edits. These alternative arrangements can then be auditioned back to back ("A-B'd") very quickly, without having to use duplicate tracks or multiple project files. Edit Playlists in a track are always auditioned in the same mix context as one another, as they all share the same automation.

Adding a New Playlist

When you create a new track, its edit playlist is empty until you record or place clips onto it. Once populated, you can create new empty playlists on the same track and begin experimenting with different arrangements of clips, or make alternative recordings.

To add a new playlist to a track:

1   From the Playlist selector on the desired track, choose the NEW command.

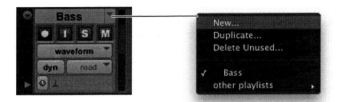

– A dialog box will open, prompting you for a playlist name.

2   You can use the default name for the playlist or type a name of your choosing, then click OK.

– A new empty playlist will appear, and the track's name will update to match the new playlist. As you create and name new playlists, they appear in the Playlist selector pop-up menu, in the order in which they were created.

Assigning a Different Playlist

Each track's pop-up Playlist Selector includes playlists created for that track in the main section of the menu, with other unused playlists from other tracks available in the Other Playlists submenu.

When you choose a different playlist, the playlist that was active will be replaced by the new playlist on that track. Any unassigned playlists become available on the playlist selectors of all other tracks.

 Track playlists can be changed during playback using the Playlist selector pop-up menu.

 Mono, stereo, and multichannel track playlists can only be recalled and assigned to the same corresponding type of audio track.

Duplicating a Playlist

When using playlists for editing and arrangement, it's more common to duplicate an existing playlist than to create a new one. Duplicating allows you to experiment with the existing track data, while retaining the original version if you decide to go back. You may create as many duplicates playlists as you like, keeping a number of different options. This can be especially useful if you are working with a producer, as you can store a number of options for the producer to choose from.

To create a duplicate playlist:

1   Display the playlist on a track you want to duplicate.

2   Choose DUPLICATE from the Playlist selector pop-up menu.

  –   In the dialog box that appears, a number is appended to the end of the original playlist name.

3   Type a new name or use the default name.

4   Click OK.

Deleting a Playlist

Alternate playlists take almost no disk space, so you don't need to delete them for space reasons, but you may still want to delete some for the sake of simplicity and organization.

To delete a playlist:

1   Make sure the playlist is not currently active on a track. You can delete playlists only if they are unused (i.e., not assigned to a track).

2   From any Playlist selector pop-up menu, choose DELETE UNUSED.

  –   A dialog box will appear allowing you to select the playlists to delete from a list of all unassigned playlists in the session.

3   Choose the playlist(s) you want to delete.

4   Click DELETE to delete the playlists.

Using the Playlist Track View

In Module 2 you used the Playlist Track View to display Playlists as additional lanes in their parent track in the Edit window.

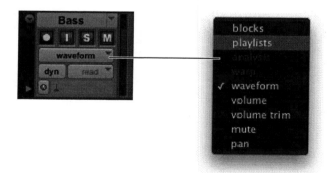

Choosing Playlist View from the Track View Selector

Playlist view can be very useful when creating and auditioning different arrangements within tracks, as in this example:

An alternative arrangement for the Bass track.

Song Arrangement

In the traditional scheme of working, a song is written and arranged before it is recorded. However, the non-linear editing available in Pro Tools makes it possible to completely rearrange the structure of a song even after all the audio and MIDI have been recorded or imported. In fact, it's not unusual for arrangement updates to continue right through the final mix, especially as mix automation can be moved with audio and MIDI in tracks. As a compositional tool, Pro Tools lets you record the basic elements of a track, and then experiment with the song structure afterwards.

This section explains several techniques for making large-scale arrangement changes, such as moving an entire chorus to a new location.

Using Cut/Insert Time Operations

In the Pro Tools 201 book, you learned about two functions of the Time Operations window that can be used for changing the overall arrangement of your song: Cut Time and Insert Time.

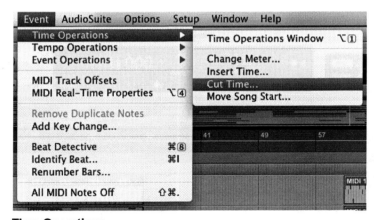

Time Operations

Cut Time

Cut Time will remove everything within a range of time across all tracks. Everything after this point in the session is shuffled earlier in time to fill the gap. Cut Time is particularly useful because it can include the rulers, so all tempo, meter, and marker information is included in the cut and the subsequent realignment of later material. Cut Time places the removed section onto the clipboard, so it can be pasted at a new time location, if needed.

To cut an entire section of a track using Cut Time:

1 [Optional] Select a range of time for cutting with the Selector. Use Grid mode to get an exact number of bars.

2 Make sure all tracks are shown by choosing SHOW ALL TRACKS from the Track List pop-up menu.

3 Choose EVENT > TIME > CUT TIME. The Time Operations window will open with the Cut Time page displayed.

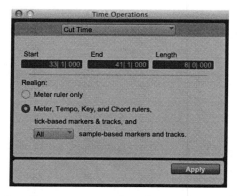

4 Confirm or enter the time values. If you previously selected a time range in the Edit window, the START, END, and LENGTH fields will already be completed.

5 From the REALIGN options, choose the rulers and tracks to affect.

6   Click APPLY. The specified range will be removed.

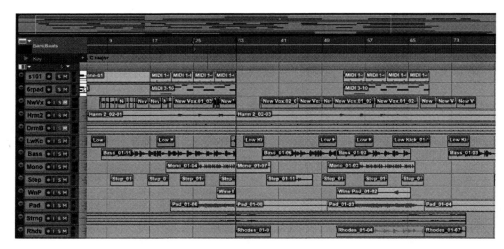

Insert Time

The Insert Time command is used to create a gap in the middle of a song and shuffle all material after the gap later in time (including selected ruler data such as tempo events).

To insert empty bars into a song:

1   Make sure all tracks are shown by choosing SHOW ALL TRACKS from the Track List pop-up menu.

2   Use the Selector to place the Edit Cursor at the point where you wish the extra bars to begin.

3   Choose EVENT > TIME > INSERT TIME. The Time Operations window will open with the Insert Time page displayed.

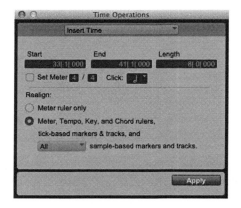

4   In the LENGTH field, type the number of bars you wish to insert.

5   From the REALIGN options, choose the rulers and tracks to affect.

6   Click APPLY. All material after the Insert point will be shuffled later by the number of bars specified.

Selecting, Copying, and Pasting Across all Tracks

After using the Cut Time operation detailed above, you can paste the cut section to a new location. All the tempo, meter, marker, and key signature information can be preserved, and you can have the remainder of the song shuffle to make room for the pasted section.

Pasting after using Cut Time

The Cut Time operation places all removed material on the clipboard, ready for pasting to a new location.

To paste to a new location after using Cut Time:

1   Make sure all tracks are shown by choosing SHOW ALL TRACKS from the Track List pop-up menu.

2   Drop the Edit Cursor across all tracks at the point you wish to paste the cut section. This is achieved by clicking in the strip between the tracks and the rulers in the Edit Window. If desired, you can use Grid mode to make sure your cursor is on a bar line.

3   Add the cursor to the Conductor rulers by shift-clicking on each with the Selector or simply dragging upwards after making your initial selection. If you don't do this, tempo and meter events, markers, and key change events will not be affected, which could put them out of sync with track contents.

4   Switch to SHUFFLE edit mode.

5   Choose EDIT > PASTE, or type COMMAND+V (Mac) or CTRL+V (Windows). Everything you previously cut will be pasted, starting at the cursor location. Because you are in Shuffle mode, all subsequent material will move later in time.

Copying all Tracks

The Time Operations window has no Copy Time function, but it is still possible to copy a whole section to another location, instead of just moving it. One option is to use the Cut Time procedure outlined above, and to immediately paste the cut section back into its original location. Another option is to simply select across all tracks (as you do when pasting) and use the COPY command.

To copy across all tracks:

1   Make sure all tracks are shown by choosing SHOW ALL TRACKS from the Track List pop-up menu.

2   Select a time range across all tracks and rulers by clicking and dragging in the gray strip between the tracks and rulers. All tracks will automatically be selected when you drag in this strip; however, you will also need to drag upwards to include the rulers.

3   Choose EDIT > COPY, or type COMMAND+C (Mac) or CTRL+C (Windows).

You can now follow the procedure for Pasting, as outlined above.

Repeating a Song Section (Duplicate Time)

Often you might want to repeat or loop an entire section of your song. Using the above procedure you can easily achieve this with Copy and Paste in Shuffle Edit mode. However, you can also follow steps 1 and 2 of the previous outline, then simply choose EDIT > DUPLICATE.

Using Nested Clip Groups for Arrangement

Pro Tools allows you to have clip groups nested within clip groups, with no limit on how many layers deep you can go. This can be used to your advantage when trying out song arrangements, as you can temporarily group sections of your song and move them around easily.

 These techniques do not move events on the rulers, so they need to be used with caution in sessions with tempo, meter, and key changes.

In this screenshot, a song has been divided into clip groups that span all tracks:

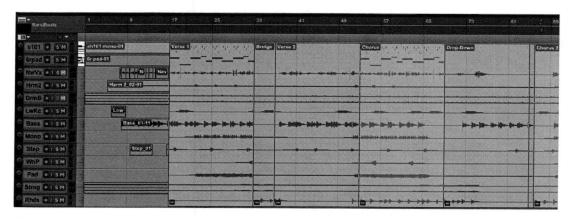

The clip groups can be rearranged (in Shuffle mode), copied and pasted, or duplicated to tryout different options. Once an arrangement has been decided upon, the clips can be Ungrouped. You can then tidy the song up, by trimming and applying crossfades where necessary, as described in Module 5.

Crossfading Grouped Clips

Clip groups can have fades and crossfades just like regular clips. Fades only apply to audio clips—MIDI clips contained by clip groups cannot have fades. In addition to crossfading between two clip groups, you can also crossfade between a clip group and ungrouped audio clips.

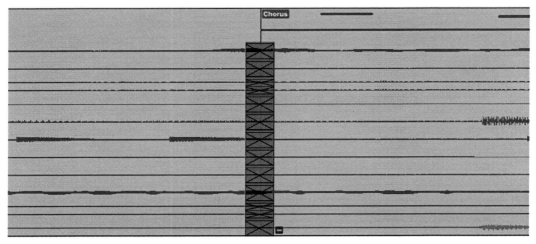

A crossfade between clip groups

 Ungrouping a clip group removes any clip group-level fades or crossfades. However, fades and crossfades are restored by the Regroup command.

Review Questions

1   How would you go about creating a snapshot of all open windows in your session, including their sizes and locations? Which window cannot be included? (See "Window Configurations" on page 194.)

2   How many Window Configurations total can Pro Tools store in a session? How can they be shared with other sessions? (See "Window Configurations" on page 194.)

3   How can you recall Window Configuration 2 using the numeric keypad? (See "Recalling Window Configurations" on page 197.)

4   What is the keyboard shortcut for displaying the Window Configuration List? (See "Window Configuration List" on page 194.)

5   Describe the process of linking a Window Configuration to a Memory Location. (See "Storing Window Configurations in Memory Locations" on page 198.)

6   Describe two ways to activate the Replace Clip command. What modifier(s) would you hold to use the drag-and-drop method? (See "The Replace Clip Command" on page 199.)

7 What are some of the options for fitting a clip when using the Replace Clip command? (See "The Replace Clip Command" on page 199.)

8 What are the Trigger Threshold sliders used for in SoundReplacer? Why are there three? (See "Trigger Threshold" on page 203.)

9 Why might you want to duplicate a playlist? How would you do so? (See "Duplicating a Playlist" on page 206.)

10 How many different Edit playlists can you have on an audio track? How many different automation playlists can you have of a given type (such as Volume automation)? (See "Playlist Editing" on page 205.)

11 When copying and pasting across all tracks in a session, why it is important to include the rulers in your selection? Why isn't this a consideration when using the Cut Time and Insert Time operations? (i.e., How would you achieve the same result using these operations?) (See "Selecting, Copying, and Pasting Across all Tracks" on page 211.)

12 Discuss some considerations for crossfading clip groups. (See "Crossfading Grouped Clips" on page 214.)

Exercise 6 Arrangement

Objectives: • Use various techniques, including Cut/Insert Time, to re-arrange a song.

Approximate Completion Time: 40 minutes.

Scenario

Your task in this session is to take the finished (but un-mixed) 210M session and create a radio edit that is significantly shorter than the original arrangement.

Getting Started

Open the session:

1 The session for this exercise can be found in the 210M PT10 Exercise 6 folder, in the location specified by your instructor (such as Audio Drive: 210M PT10 Class Files: 210M PT10 Exercise 6: 210M PT10 Exercise 6.ptx).

2 If the Missing Files dialog box opens, choose Manually Find and Relink; the files are located in the 210M PT10 Exercise Master folder in the location specified by your instructor (such as Audio Drive: PT210M PT10 Class Files: 210M PT10 Exercise Master).

3 Save the session to the location specified by your instructor, with the name <your initials>210M Exercise 6.ptx.

Take a few moments to familiarize yourself with the arrangement and what is on the various tracks.

Create a Radio Edit [Challenge]

Your challenge is to reduce the song to around 3.5 minutes in length. Feel free to use any of the techniques you have learned in this or other courses, but pay particular attention to the Cut Time and Insert Time Operations discussed in Chapter 7.

Techniques to Use

Take the opportunity to try the following techniques:

- Using the Cut/Insert Time Operation
- Duplicating across all tracks
- Creating Clip Groups from song structures (e.g. a whole chorus, or large section of drums & beats)
- Using Playlists to make safety copies when trying out ideas.

Requirements for the Arrangement

You may do whatever you wish with the arrangement, but here are some requirements to get you started:

- The finished track should be three and a half minutes long, give or take 10 seconds.
- This is not a remix exercise: use the existing elements of the song; don't add new parts.

- Start by using the Cut Time operation to remove 8 bars from the Introduction. Be careful not to lose the early piano notes that come in ahead of the first bar.
- Bring the Bass part in at bar 17.
- Try cutting the first chorus in half.
- Try cutting the breakdown section in half.
- Try reducing the outro.

Tidy up Your Edits

After making large changes, such as when using Cut Time, make sure to clean up the new transitions that are left between parts of the song. This may require creating overlaps by trimming out some tracks so that the song continues to flow smoothly. You will probably need to rework some sections of the vocal tracks.

The following two images show an example solution to this exercise. The first image shows the session after rough, large-scale edits have been made. The second image is a close-up view of one of the new transitions after it has been smoothed with finer scale, track-by-track editing.

Rough, song-wide edits

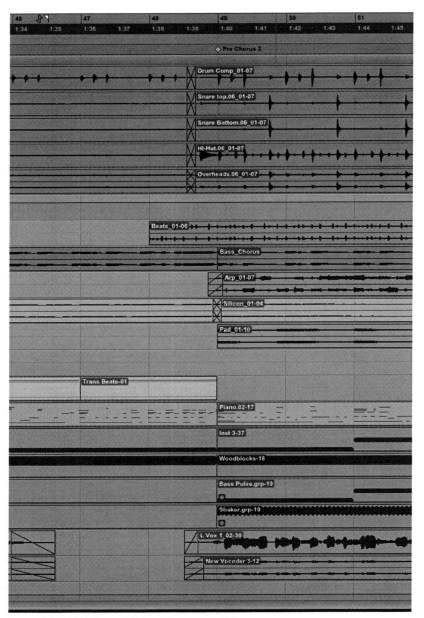

One of the new transitions after smoothing

Module 8 Mixing and Automation

In this chapter you will investigate some advanced mixing techniques.

Objectives:
- Delay compensation and MIDI
- Delay compensation and Hardware Inserts
- Writing static mixer automation
- Trim automation
- Variable Stereo Pan Depth

Introduction

In this chapter, we examine some mixing concepts that are particularly important when you are composing music with Pro Tools. We also introduce some new automation features. First, we consider how delay compensation relates to MIDI recording and synchronization. Then we look at two complementary techniques that allow you to write mixer settings to different sections of your songs. Lastly, we discuss some of the features of Auto Trim mode, an automation mode that allows you to make adjustments to existing mix automation.

Delay Compensation and MIDI Offsets

In this section, you'll learn how delay compensation relates to MIDI and Instrument Tracks, and how to keep MIDI and audio in sync.

MIDI Track Timing Adjustment

The Pro Tools Delay Compensation feature is used to preserve timing between multiple audio tracks as they run through different digital signal processing paths with varying amounts of delay. Delay compensation can also have implications for the timing of MIDI-based material, depending on what instruments are playing the MIDI parts and how those instruments are being monitored. MIDI hardware instruments that are being monitored through a Pro Tools Aux Input or Instrument Track will be compensated along with other tracks, but other considerations also apply.

MIDI Recording Adjustment

Consider what happens when you record on MIDI or Instrument Tracks while Delay Compensation is active. Because you are recording against other tracks that are being delayed, you will be playing the MIDI parts late. To prevent the MIDI data from being out of sync, after each record pass, Pro Tools shifts your MIDI recordings earlier in time to compensate.

Low-Latency Recording with Virtual Instrument Plug-Ins

When a MIDI or Instrument Track that is routing MIDI data to a virtual instrument is record-enabled, Pro Tools automatically suspends Delay Compensation through the main outputs of the track hosting the virtual instrument. This allows for latency-free monitoring of the instrument plug-in during recording.

Offsetting MIDI Tracks

In addition to Pro Tools' Delay Compensation feature (which compensates for DSP-related latency), at certain times you may wish to set a MIDI timing offset for a MIDI or Instrument Track to compensate for latency associated with MIDI control:

- Hardware Instruments Monitored Outside of Pro Tools—If you are monitoring a hardware MIDI instrument through an external mixer instead of routing it through Pro Tools, you may wish to set an offset delay to match the Delay Compensation amount that Pro Tools tracks are subject to during playback.

- Non-TDM systems—If you are using a non-TDM Pro Tools system, you may wish to set a global offset to compensate for the latency incurred when monitoring external MIDI instruments through your interface.

- MIDI Transmission and Hardware Response Delays—Under some circumstances, you may wish to compensate for other latency factors, such as the response time of your MIDI instrument. Although small, these delays may be significant when you are doubling up percussive sounds, such as when adding a MIDI-triggered snare to a recorded snare. In these situations, any delay could cause a noticeable flamming or phasing.

Setting MIDI Offsets

Pro Tools provides several ways that you can adjust MIDI timing, including using a global offset, using individual track offsets, and specifying an offset with MIDI Real-Time Properties.

Global Offset

You can set a global MIDI timing adjustment in the MIDI page of the Preferences dialog box (SETUP > PREFERENCES). This offset affects playback of MIDI and Instrument Tracks with respect to Audio tracks; it does not alter how MIDI data is displayed in the Edit window.

This offset is mainly used to compensate for throughput latency when monitoring through a non-TDM Pro Tools system. In such a case, you should set this to a negative number of samples equal to the Hardware Buffer Size displayed in the Playback Engine settings.

Global MIDI Playback Offset (–10,000 to 10,000): 0 samples

Track Offsets

Choosing EVENT > MIDI TRACK OFFSETS opens a window where you can adjust tracks individually. Offset values are entered in samples (by double-clicking the number displayed in the SAMPLE OFFSET column); the offsets are translated into milliseconds based on the sample rate of the session.

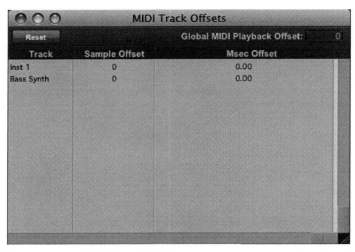

You can use MIDI track offsets to compensate for the delay time that a MIDI device introduces when triggering an event. For example, samplers and synthesizers commonly require at least 5 ms to trigger a MIDI note. Delay times vary depending on the device and the sound or patch being triggered.

Real-Time Properties Offsets

MIDI and Instrument Tracks can also be delayed or advanced using Real-Time Properties for each track. This is useful when adjusting the delay by ear (e.g. when syncing doubled-up sounds), and also provides a much larger range of offset times (up to 2000ms).

For the purposes of delay compensation, you would use MIDI Real-Time Properties in much the same way as MIDI track offsets.

Note: The timing of MIDI data can also be affected during playback by MIDI jitter—timing variations that occur when the CPU delays playing a MIDI event due to other CPU processing that is occurring.

Note: Variation in MIDI playback timing is generally considered to be acceptable in the range of 40-50 samples, or 1 msec, in either direction.

Delay Compensation for MIDI Beat Clock

The mixer delay compensation can be applied to outgoing MIDI Beat Clock (and MIDI Time Code) by selecting the corresponding options in the MIDI page of the Preferences dialog box.

Caution: You should only choose these options when monitoring external devices through an external mixer. If you are monitoring through Pro Tools, the audio signals will be delayed as a result, and these options should not be applied.

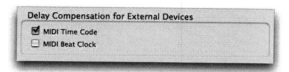

Delay options in MIDI Preferences

 These options will appear in the MIDI Preferences page only when a Delay Compensation value has been set in the Playback Engine dialog box.

MIDI Beat Clock Offsets

In addition to the global offset to correct for Delay Compensation in the mixer, you can add individual offsets to MIDI Beat Clock for any MIDI port. This allows you to fine-tune the synchronization between Pro Tools and Beat Clock slaves, adjusting for any fixed latencies.

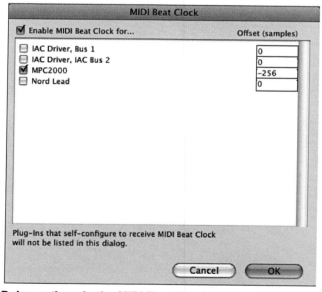

Delay options in the MIDI Beat Clock window

Offsets are entered in the same window where MIDI Beat Clock outputs are activated (Setup > MIDI > MIDI Beat Clock).

Delay Compensation and Hardware Inserts

When you use a hardware insert on a track (to route a signal to an external effects device and back via an audio interface), the signal will delayed slightly. Passing a signal through your interface incurs a delay, and additional processing latency is typically added by your outboard digital effects devices.

Note: Pro Tools' Delay Compensation automatically corrects for the latency of Avid audio interfaces.

The Hardware Insert Delay page in the I/O Setup dialog box lets you enter a value so that Pro Tools can compensate for any delay caused by passing through an external device. The throughput latency of a device may be published in its manual. If not, you may consider measuring it when configuring your studio, by sending a recorded signal from Pro Tools through the device, re-recording its return, and measuring the difference between the two waveforms.

Hardware Insert delays that are entered in the Hardware Insert Delay tab of the I/O Setup window are factored in when Delay Compensation is active.

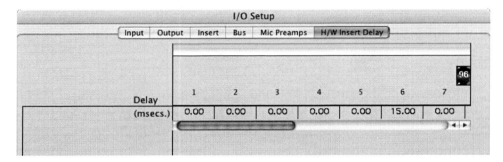

Writing Static Mixer Settings

In previous courses, you have learned various ways to record mixer automation. In most cases you have written dynamic automation, i.e. recorded real-time adjustments made to parameters on the mixer and plug-ins. The exception is in Pro Tools 201, where you were briefly introduced to the WRITE TO ALL/END/START/NEXT/PUNCH commands in the Automation window, and the WRITE TO CURRENT and WRITE TO ALL ENABLED commands in the Edit menu.

These commands all write flat parameter settings throughout a section of the session. This type of automation is sometimes referred to as Static or Snapshot Automation. A section of static automation can be as simple as a single plug-in bypass, or as complicated as a mixer-wide recall of levels, pans, sends, and plug-in settings.

There are many situations where it is appropriate to write automation in this way, for example:

- You need to change an effect's parameters at different places in the song. For example, you might have the Eleven plug-in set to a clean guitar sound at some points, but an overdriven sound at others.

- Similarly, you might want to change a virtual instrument's parameters during the song.

- You want to set the balance of lead and backing vocals differently during different song sections.

- The song has two distinctly different sections; the entire mix changes between the two movements.

Two Families of Write Commands

Before we look at some workflows, it's important to understand the distinction between the WRITE TO ALL/END/START/NEXT/PUNCH commands in the Automation window, and the WRITE TO CURRENT / WRITE TO ALL ENABLED commands in the Edit menu. Although they are similarly named, and can be used for similar purposes, they are not the same commands, and have a number of differences.

The Write commands in the Automation window (left), and the Edit > Automation commands.

WRITE TO ALL/END/START/NEXT/PUNCH can only be used during playback. These write automation to all parameters that are currently writing or (as you'll learn shortly) parameters isolated in Preview mode.

To recap what you learned in 201:

- WRITE TO ALL writes the current settings of all currently writing mixer/plug-in parameters to the entire timeline selection (or the whole session if there's no timeline selection).

- WRITE TO END writes the current settings of all currently writing mixer/plug-in parameters from the current time to the end of the timeline selection (or to the end of the session if there's no timeline selection).

- WRITE TO START writes the current settings of all currently writing mixer/plug-in parameters from the current time to the start of the timeline selection (or to the beginning of the session if there's no timeline selection).

- WRITE TO NEXT writes the current settings of all currently writing mixer/plug-in parameters from the current time to the next automation breakpoint on each automation playlist.

- WRITE TO PUNCH writes the current settings of all currently writing mixer/plug-in parameters from the current time back to the point that they began writing.

By contrast, the WRITE TO CURRENT and WRITE TO ALL ENABLED commands (and their variants) can be used in stop or during playback, and they only write to parameters on tracks containing an edit selection, and within the current edit selection's time range. These commands are considered automation playlist edit commands, and are unaffected by track automation modes.

- WRITE TO CURRENT writes the setting(s) of the currently displayed automation playlist(s), within the edit selection. This means that only one parameter can be written per track. For this reason, it is much more common to use WRITE TO ALL ENABLED.

- WRITE TO ALL ENABLED writes the current settings of all automation parameters within the current edit selection, except for parameter types that are disabled in the Automation Window.

Summary of Differences between the Write Commands:

Write to All/End/Start/Next/Punch	Write to Current/All Enabled
Located in the Automation Window	Located in the Edit > Automation menu
Dedicated button cluster on D-Control/D-Command	In Soft Key section of D-Control/D-Command
Write to currently writing/isolated parameters	Write to the displayed parameter/all parameters
Write within the Timeline selection on all tracks	Write within the Edit Selection, and only to tracks that contain the Edit Selection
Not active if automation suspended	Can still write when automation suspended
Will only write to tracks in a Write, Latch, Touch or Touch/Latch modes (with or without Trim enabled)	Will write to track selections even if the track is in Off or Read mode

In the following pages you'll learn how to use both of these sets of features to write mixer settings to sections of your song and how to determine which method is appropriate in different situations.

Workflows for Writing Static Mixer Settings

Consider one of the examples given at the start of this section: a guitar track that requires two different treatments in the song. One solution would be to cut the guitar recording to two different tracks. However, this means doubling up on plug-ins. A more elegant solution (especially in situations where you need to make changes to several tracks) is to change settings through automation.

Basic Outline

The basic workflow for this technique is similar in all situations:

1   Use AUTO PREVIEW MODE to configure mixer and plug-in settings without disturbing the existing mix or automation.

2   Write the new settings.

Step 1 is the same for all our examples; step 2 varies depending on the situation (and, to a certain extent, personal preference).

Preview Mode

Preview mode can be switched on and off in the AUTOMATION window, or in the AUTOMATION > ACTIONS Soft Key page on ICON worksurfaces.

Preview Mode activated from the Automation window

When Preview mode is active, mixer or plug-in automation plays back as normal. However, as soon as you touch any control, that parameter becomes "isolated" from its automation. The parameter will not play back or write automation, and will remain un-automated until you exit Preview mode or invoke one of the Write commands.

This is useful because it allows you to experiment with mixer and plug-in settings while Pro Tools plays back, without writing automation and without fighting with any automation that already exists for those parameters. Preview also inhibits changes to the automation graphs of un-automated parameters on write-enabled tracks, which is not the case if you simply Suspend automation or switch the tracks to Off mode. This means your previous mix can be completely recovered just by exiting Preview.

Writing Isolated Parameters

Any changes you make in Preview mode can be discarded by exiting Preview, or you can choose to write the new settings as automation in a number of different ways.

Workflow 1: Preview and Write

The picture below shows the guitar track from our example. For most of this section the guitarist picks a clean arpeggio, but between bars 57 and 65 she strums. You've set up a sound that works during the picked sections, using EQ, Dynamics, and the Eleven amp simulator plug-in. However, you'd like a louder, more overdriven sound during the 8 bars of strumming.

Guitar Track with Markers indicating the sections

To write new mix settings to the 8 bar section:

1   Select the 8-bar section.

– Depending on which Write command you intend to use, you'll either need a Timeline or Edit Selection. If Link Timeline and Edit Selection is on, there is no distinction.

2   Put the track into Touch or Latch mode.

3   Engage Auto Preview mode.

4   Enable Loop Playback.

5   Press Play.

6   While Pro Tools plays back, adjust all the necessary mixer and plug-in settings to get the sound you need for the section. This may just be the Eleven Plug-in, or it may also include the track fader, send levels, EQ, and even Reverb or Delay settings and levels of return tracks.

The original Eleven settings (left) and the changed settings for the 8-bar section.

– When you are happy with how the mix sounds during this section, you are ready to commit it to automation.

7   Check that all the types of automation (Volume, Plug-in, Send Volume, etc.) you have changed are Write Enabled in the Automation window.

8   You now have two options for writing the automation:

– Option 1: Press the MANUAL WRITE TO ALL button in the Automation window (or on D-Control/D-Command.

Every parameter that you've touched or moved since entering Preview mode will be written at its current level to the Timeline Selection. If you've changed parameters on more than one track, such as the guitar track and a reverb return, automation will be written on all these tracks.

– Option 2: Choose EDIT > AUTOMATION > WRITE TO ALL ENABLED, or press OPTION+COMMAND+/ (Mac) or CTRL+ALT+/ (Windows).

Every mixer/plug-in parameter (whether moved or not) will be written at its current level to the Edit Selection. If you've changed parameters on more than one track, you need to ensure that the Edit Selection is on all the tracks that you want to write to. This may require Shift-clicking in each track that automation is to be written to.

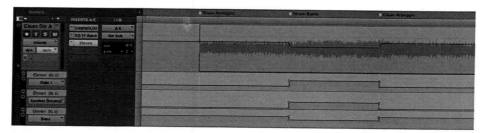

Automation graphs indicating the new mix settings during the 8-bar section

9   Exit Auto PREVIEW mode.

You can test that the procedure was successful by playing through the boundary between the two sections and watching the mixer/plug-in parameters snap to new positions.

Choosing between Option 1 and Option 2

Which option should you choose at Step 8? The results are very similar. In either case everything you changed about the mix is written as automation to the relevant section. The main difference is that parameters that you didn't touch are also written if you go for option 2.

Given that the MANUAL WRITE TO ALL command is faster, safer, and requires no Edit selection, Option 1 tends to be the first choice. However, the difference that needs considering is how un-automated parameters are treated by the two commands.

Because MANUAL WRITE TO ALL does not write break-points to all parameters in the selection, unautomated parameters remain unaffected after your write pass. This means that some mixer changes you make later while working on another part of the song could change the way the track sounds during the section you wrote. For example, there may have been settings in Eleven that sounded right at their default setting so you didn't adjust them while in Preview mode. If you change any of these settings later in the song, they will be changed throughout the whole track.

On the other hand, WRITE TO ALL ENABLED anchors all parameters at the selected range boundaries, including parameters that had previously been unautomated. The advantage of this is that it guarantees that the tracks you were working on will always sound the same at this section, regardless of subsequent changes elsewhere in the timeline. However, writing to parameters you've not touched risks overwriting dynamic automation within the selection.

If you're aware of all these issues, you can select the appropriate action for the situation, and mitigate the potential problems of each method. For example, before using MANUAL WRITE TO ALL, you can touch additional parameters to ensure they are included in the automation. Conversely, when using WRITE TO ALL ENABLED you can avoid overwriting your dynamic automation by careful use of the Write Enable buttons in the Automation window.

Workflow 2: Preview and Punch

In Workflow 1, you found the settings you want, then wrote them instantaneously to a section of your song. Punch Preview offers an alternative way of working, in which you adjust settings in Auto Preview mode, then write the settings in real time. The PUNCH PREVIEW button can be found next to the PREVIEW button in the Automation window. Punch Preview can also be actuated from the AUTOMATION > ACTIONS Soft Key page on ICON worksurfaces

The Punch Preview button

There are two different ways of using Punch Preview:

1. Punch-in during Playback

While you are playing back in Auto Preview, you can immediately commence writing isolated parameters as automation at any time. This allows you to work without setting a precise timeline or edit selection, and to hear the transition from one section to another as you write. For example, as you listen to a section of your mix you can switch into Preview mode, adjust some settings, rewind to a few bars before the point where the mix changes, then manually punch in at the desired location.

To write automation on-the-fly with Punch Preview:

1   Enter Auto PREVIEW mode and adjust parameters during playback.

2   During playback, click the PUNCH PREVIEW button.

–   Isolated parameters on tracks in Touch, Latch, or Write mode will begin writing. Tracks in Touch will be switched to Latch, to facilitate the Punch.

Obviously there's little advantage to punching in halfway through the section you're mixing, so usually you would move the play position back to an earlier point. While in Preview, you can freely move the play position without losing the settings of your isolated parameters.

2. Cue up and Punch

Instead of punching in on-the-fly, you can Punch Preview while the transport is stopped. Isolated parameters will begin writing when you press Play. This option is often preferable, as it allows you to cue up the start point of the automation precisely. So why would you do this instead of just selecting the whole range and using one of the Write commands? This method allows you to write a basic static mix while you make dynamic adjustments at the same time, and can work well with linear mixing tasks, such as working through a song riding the levels.

An example:

A session has several backing vocal tracks which need a lot of volume automation to work in the various sections of the song. This will require a mixture of static balance changes and dynamic fader rides. Playing through the session, you set up a balance that works for the first part of the song. When you reach the next section you activate Auto Preview mode and set new levels. When you're ready, you park Pro Tools' play position at the start of the second section, press Punch Preview, then start playback. The basic static mix is written as you play back, and you continue to make dynamic adjustments as you listen through. At each new section you repeat the process.

To Punch Preview from a "standing start":

1   Enter Auto Preview mode and adjust parameters during playback.

2   Stop the transport.

3   Position the Playback cursor at the point where you wish to start writing the Previewed settings.

4   Click Punch Preview.

– All isolated parameters on tracks in Touch, Latch, or Write mode will become primed for writing automation. Tracks in Touch mode will be switched to Latch.

5   Press Play.

– The isolated parameters will begin writing from the Play position.

Note: Punching Previewed mix settings in Stop is similar to using Pro Tools' "Latch Prime in Stop" feature, which is described in Pro Tools 310M. Latch Prime in Stop does not need to be active in order for Punch Preview to work while in Stop.

Trim Automation

Pro Tools' Trim automation modes allow you to proportionally scale existing volume automation, retaining the contours of dynamic automation as desired. This is useful when you have already recorded fader rides, but later find you need to adjust the balance at certain points in your mix (or across the whole mix).

When writing automation in Trim mode, fader moves write *relative* rather than *absolute* values. The existing automation data is changed by the amount of increase or decrease (or the *delta* value) indicated by the faders.

Trim automation exists as a separate automation graph in its own right, modifying the main volume automation in real time. In the following screenshot, Trim automation is displayed in Yellow, and modifies the main Volume automation (Black) to produce the audible result (called the "Composite Playlist"), indicated in Blue.

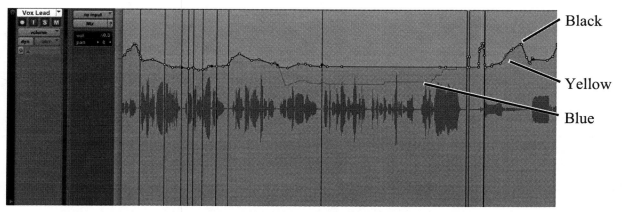

Volume (Black) and Volume Trim (Yellow) automation graphs, the Composite Playlist in Blue.

Varieties of Trim Mode

Trim mode is not an independent mode like Latch or Touch. Instead, each of the primary writing modes can be switched into Trim, i.e. you can be in Latch Trim, Write Trim, etc.

To activate an automation mode for trimming automation:

1   Click the AUTOMATION MODE SELECTOR on the track you want to trim, and choose TRIM, or press the channel's TRIM button on your control surface.

2   Click the AUTOMATION MODE SELECTOR on the track again or press the channel's AUTO on your control surface and select the desired automation mode (Touch, Latch, Touch/Latch, or Write) for your trimming operations.

The primary automation mode you select determines the way in which automation is written during a pass. For example, if you choose Touch Trim mode, Trim automation is only written while a fader or send level control is touched.

Each of the Trim automation modes is detailed in Table 1 on the next page.

Table 1 Pro Tools Trim Automation Modes

Automation Mode	Automation Trimming Starts	Automation Trimming Stops	Usage Examples
read trim	Automation play ONLY mode. When playback begins, trimming can be auditioned but no automation is actually written.	n/a	Audition and rehearse mode for balance changes with no automation written.
touch trim	Trimming starts when volume or send level controls are modified.	Trimming stops when a modified control is released, with the parameter returning to the previous Trim value based on the AutoMatch Time preference.	Trimming the volume automation of a vocal track up 2 dB during the chorus of a song only, and then automatically returning to the original automation.
latch trim	Trimming starts when volume or send level controls are modified (can be pre-armed if Latch Prime in Stop mode is enabled).	Trimming stops for all modified parameters when playback stops.	Trimming several faders at once. Allows faders to be 'set and left'. Useful in combination with Write to All/Selection.
touch/latch trim	Trimming starts when volume or send level controls are modified.	Volume trimming stops as per Touch Mode; Send Level behaves as in Latch mode.	Lets you 'set and leave' a reverb send trim, while dropping in and out on the main fader.
write trim	Volume and send level trimming starts immediately at playback, using the current delta value.	Volume and send level trimming stops when playback stops.	Rarely used. Can be used for overwriting previous Trim passes with new values.

Writing Trim Automation

When you write automation in any of the Trim modes, the volume and send level faders are disengaged from displaying and following existing automation data. Faders are automatically positioned at 0 dB, where no trimming occurs (they start with a delta value of zero).

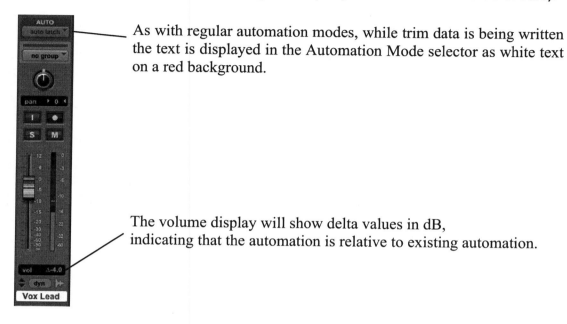

As with regular automation modes, while trim data is being written the text is displayed in the Automation Mode selector as white text on a red background.

The volume display will show delta values in dB, indicating that the automation is relative to existing automation.

Viewing Trim Automation

Volume and Send Level Trim automation is stored on separate automation graphs (playlists) and can be viewed directly in the Edit window. Trim automation is also shown in the background when the parameter it is affecting is viewed in a track (as shown in an earlier screenshot).

To display trim automation:

1 Click the Track View Selector on the track whose trim automation you wish to view.

2 Choose either VOLUME TRIM (for main fader trim) or LEVEL TRIM from a Send sub-menu.

Volume Trim chosen from the Track View Selector

Coalescing Trim Automation

Although Trim automation can be stored indefinitely as a separate graph, you can choose to write its effects to the main automation playlist. Known as coalescing, this process effectively results in the main automation graph becoming identical to the blue composite playlist shown in the previous screenshot. After you coalesce Trim automation, the Trim playlist resets to a flat 0dB graph again, providing a fresh starting point for any subsequent trimming.

Trim automation can be coalesced or committed to the main automation playlist in a variety of ways, as determined by a preference setting (SETUP > PREFERENCES > MIXING tab). Pro Tools provides the following coalesce options:

- After Every Pass—Trim moves are automatically applied to the main automation playlist as soon as the transport is stopped at the end of an automation pass.

- On Exiting Trim Mode—Trim moves are stored in the Trim automation playlist until you take the track out of Trim mode. The Trim automation playlist can be modified and edited until you exit Trim mode, at which point it is applied to the main automation playlist.

- Manually—Trim moves are stored in the Trim automation playlist until being committed with the Coalesce Trim Automation command (TRACK > COALESCE TRIM AUTOMATION). The Trim automation playlist can be modified and edited until being manually coalesced.

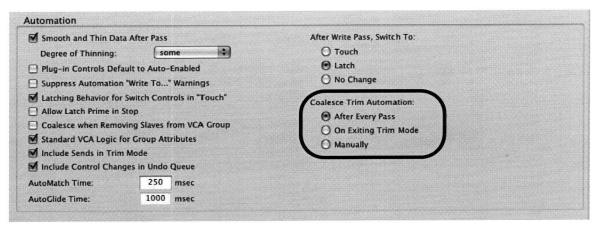

Trim automation preferences

You can also manually clear or coalesce all Trim automation from trim playlists on a track.

To clear Trim automation from a track:

- Right-click on the Track name in the Edit or Mix windows, and choose CLEAR TRIM AUTOMATION. All Trim automation for the main volume and send levels will be cleared.

To coalesce Trim automation to the main Automation playlists on a track:

- Right-click on the Track name in the Edit or Mix windows, and choose COALESCE TRIM AUTOMATION. All Trim automation for the main volume and send levels will be coalesced with the main automation graphs.

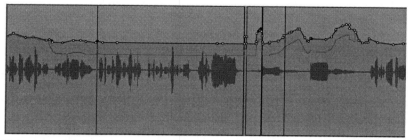

Volume graph before coalescing trim automation

Volume graph after coalescing trim automation

Variable Stereo Pan Depth

A feature introduced in Pro Tools 9.0 lets you select one of four pan depth choices for stereo output paths: -2.5 dB, -3.0 dB, -4.5 dB, or -6.0 dB. The Pan Depth setting determines the amount of signal attenuation used when a track that is routed to a stereo output is panned to center.

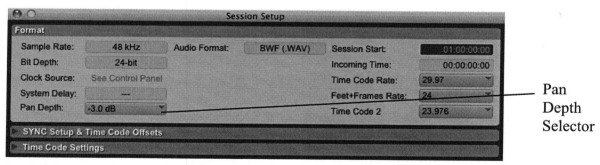

Session Setup window

To set the pan depth, open the Session Setup window (Setup > Session) and select the desired option from the Pan Depth selector.

Caution: On Pro Tools|HD systems only, if the Stereo Mixer plug-in is installed in the plug-ins folder, the Pan Depth setting defaults to -2.5 dB and cannot be changed. Move the Stereo Mixer plug-in to the Plug-Ins (Unused) folder to be able to change the Pan Depth setting.

Note: The Surround Mixer requires slightly more DSP resources than the Stereo Mixer. Consequently, if you plan to use the Pan Depth of -2.5 dB, you may want to use the Stereo Mixer plug-in.

Stereo Pan Depth Options

The following pan depth options are available.

- **-2.5:** Used to be the standard stereo Pan Depth setting in Pro Tools 8.0.x and lower. When opening Pro Tools 8.0.x session in Pro Tools 8.1 or later, this is the default option.

- **-3.0:** The industry standard for surround mixers and many consoles. This is the default setting of new sessions in Pro Tools 8.1 and later..

- **-4.5:** The standard for many British analog consoles.

- **-6.0:** The standard for full mono compatibility.

Caution: For greater than stereo formats (such as 5.1), all surround output panning is fixed at -3.0 dB. The variable pan depth options are only available for stereo outputs.

Pan Law

Consider a mono signal that is playing out of a single speaker at a given level (we'll call it unity gain). If we add a second speaker playing the same signal at the same level (also unit gain), we will increase the overall volume of the output signal (beyond unity gain). That is exactly what we are doing when we place a mono signal in the center of a stereo mix with a balance control (or a pan control with no center attenuation). This observation has a led to a well-known recording and mixing principle called the *Pan Law*.

The Pan Law states that any audio signal of equal amplitude and phase that is played in both channels of a stereo system will increase loudness by up to 6.02 dB, subject to the accuracy of the acoustic summing provided by the system and the acoustic properties of the listening space.

A similar increase can occur with stereo signals when both channels are panned to center without attenuation, depending on the degree of correlation in the program material between the left and right channels -- non-correlated signals won't cause an increase, while signals that are closely correlated will cause a corresponding increase, proportionate to the degree of correlation (or phase coherence) in the left and right channels.

Pan Depth Settings

To prevent this "artificial" increase in amplitude, Pro Tools attenuates the center position of its pan controls, based on the selected Pan Depth setting. The question becomes, which Pan Depth setting will be the best at keeping levels consistent as you pan across the stereo field? Unfortunately, there is no universal "best" option for Pan Depth, as the amount of signal increase at the center position depends on multiple factors, including the tuning of the listening space and the program material in question.

With the -3 dB stereo Pan Depth option, a mono signal that outputs at unity gain when panned hard left or hard right will be attenuated by 3 dB when panned in the center. This is the most common setting used in the industry. It represents a compromise between no "panoramic" perception (like a balance control, or 0 dB pan depth) and a fully mono-compatible setting.

Although -3 dB is common, there is no industry standard for pan depth. As a result, different DAWs (Logic, Nuendo, etc.) use different pan depths, as do different consoles. Having different choices for pan depth in Pro Tools makes it easier to move mixes between Pro Tools and other systems, and also lets users select the Pan Depth that works best for their environment.

Note: The pan depth setting is saved as part of the session file.

Review Questions

1   Describe the effect on timing of recording MIDI while Automatic Delay Compensation is active. How does Pro Tools address the associated issues? (See "MIDI Recording Adjustment" on page 222.)

2   Name three ways to create a MIDI offset. (See "Setting MIDI Offsets" on page 223.)

3   Why might you want to set up MIDI Beat Clock offsets? (See "MIDI Beat Clock Offsets" on page 225.)

4   What are the main differences between the Write commands found in the Automation window and the ones in the EDIT > AUTOMATION menu? (See "Two Families of Write Commands" on page 227.)

5   What automation playlists are affected by the WRITE TO CURRENT command? (See "Two Families of Write Commands" on page 227.)

6   What automation playlists are affected by the WRITE TO ALL ENABLED command? Is the effect limited to automation playlists that are currently writing automation? (See "Two Families of Write Commands" on page 227.)

7 What are the advantages of using Auto Preview mode compared to Auto Suspend? (See "Preview Mode" on page 229.)

8 What are some situations where you might use Trim automation? (See "Trim Automation" on page 235.)

9 What color is used to display Trim automation playlists? (See "Trim Automation" on page 235.)

10 What does coalescing Trim automation do? (See "Coalescing Trim Automation" on page 238.)

Exercise 7 Automation

This exercise covers various automation techniques that are useful when working with audio in a music production environment.

Objectives:
- Use Trim Automation mode to make adjustments to an existing mix.
- Create a Static Automation change in the middle of a mix.

Approximate Completion Time: 40 minutes.

Scenario

In this Exercise you will play the role of a mix engineer with several updates to make to a mix. You will be making some adjustments to the vocal tracks in the 210M session, using Trim and Static automation techniques from the previous chapter.

Getting Started

Open your session for Exercise 7:

1   The session for this exercise can be found in the 210M PT10 Exercise 7 folder, in the location specified by your instructor (such as Audio Drive: 210M PT10 Class Files: 210M PT10 Exercise 7: 210M PT10 Exercise 7.ptx).

2   If the Missing Files dialog box opens, choose Manually Find and Relink; the files are located in the 210M PT10 Exercise Master folder in the location specified by your instructor (such as Audio Drive: PT210M PT10 Class Files: 210M PT10 Exercise Master).

3   Save the session to the location specified by your instructor, with the name <your initials>210M Exercise 7.ptx.

Listen to the Vocals

There are two vocal tracks in the session: the clean vocal comp and a recorded vocoder effect generated from the same vocals. The tracks have volume automation "rides" which have been added to keep the vocals at a similar level relative to both the quiet and loud parts of the backing track. You will be making some additional adjustments to this existing mix data.

1. Adjust the Level during the Last Section [Guided]

You have identified a problem in the last section (marked as "Chorus 3" from Bar 122). From the first line of soloed vocals "And When You Dream..." to the last line in the Outro, the vocal is too quiet and gets lost in the mix. Use Trim automation to push the vocals during this section.

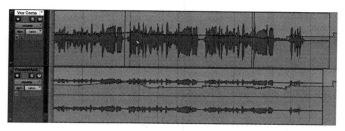

1   Enable Trim Mode on the Vox Comp and Vocoder Alt 2 tracks, and leave the automation mode as Latch.

2   Open the Pro Tools Preferences, switch to the MIXING tab, and set the Coalesce Trim Automation setting to MANUALLY.

3   Park Pro Tools at a point before Chorus 3, and begin playback.

4   Just before the music drops out and the solo line "And When You Dream..." comes in, push the faders up a few dB to make more impact at this moment in the song. You can watch the Master Fader meters to see how much headroom is available. If you don't like the result, simply Stop, press Undo, and try again.

5   Continue playback through Chorus 3, with the faders pushed to keep the vocal prominent in the mix.

2. Adjust the Overall Balance [Guided]

In this step, you will adjust the overall balance between the Vox Comp and the Vocoder Alt 2 tracks. To do this, you will use both Trim mode and the Manual Write to All command.

1   Coalesce the Trim automation you created in Step 1, by right-clicking on each vocal track's name plate in turn and choosing COALESCE TRIM AUTOMATION.

2   Begin playback from the start of the song, with no timeline selection.

3   Adjust the balance between the two vocal tracks so that the Vocoder becomes much more prominent. Try to keep the overall vocal level the same by cutting the dry vocal by the same amount that you boost the vocoded vocal. You don't need to play right through the song, and you don't need to get the faders into the right position before the vocals come in: simply set the new fader trim levels, leave Pro Tools playing back, and move to the next step...

4   Press the Manual Write to All button (either on D-Command/D-Control or in the Automation window). The automation on the tracks will be trimmed for the whole song.

3. Create a Static Automation Change

This task is to automate a static mixer change during the breakdown section before the final chorus. You will change the vocal balance so that only the dry Vocal Comp track is heard, and you will add an echo effect by automating the existing Vox Delay track.

1   Disable Trim mode on the two vocal tracks.

2   Switch the Vox Delay track to Latch mode.

3   Select the vocal during the Breakdown section (bars 99-122). You will need to switch to Slip mode to make an accurate selection that does not overlap any other sections of vocal. If LINK TIMELINE AND EDIT SELECTION has been disabled, be sure that the selection you make is a timeline selection.

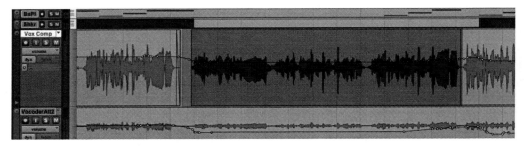

4   Engage PREVIEW mode.

5   Enable Loop Playback mode, and begin playback.

6   Set the Vocode vocal fader to minimum, and boost the dry vocal.

7   Adjust the Vox Comp's Send B (Vox Delay Send) to around 0dB.

8   Open the AIR Dynamic Delay plug-in on the Vox Delay Track.

3. Create a Static Automation Change

9   Adjust the settings to create a Slap effect, such as in the image below. Switch off the Sync button and select a delay of around 60ms.

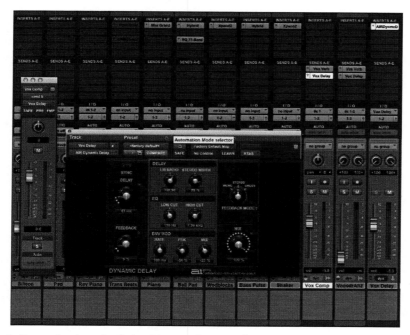

10   Adjust the level of the Vox Delay track to taste.

11   When everything sounds as you want it, press the MANUAL WRITE TO ALL button (either on D-Command/D-Control or in the Automation window). This must be done during playback. All the changes you've made will be written as automation.

12   Disable Preview mode.

13   Rewind the track to before the breakdown section and press Play. You should see all your settings recalled during the section.

Module 9　Printing Your Mix

This chapter covers several advanced options for delivering your final mix.

Objectives:

- Export your mix as an mp3 or WMA file

- Send your mix to more than one device using multiple Pro Tools outputs

Introduction

It is easy to overlook the work that comes after the final mix is completed, but delivering the fruits of your labour for approval or mastering, etc., will be an important part of your job as a Pro Tools Operator.

In this chapter, you'll learn how to deliver your mix as an MP3/WMA file. You'll then learn how to send your mix to multiple interface outputs.

MP3/WMA Export

MP3 (MPEG-1 Layer 3) and WMA (Windows Media Audio) are both compressed file formats commonly used for downloading and streaming media over the internet, and for storage on portable audio players. Due to its ability to support lossless compression and surround options, Windows Media Audio can also be used in professional environments for sending audio between locations. You can either export a whole mix to these formats using Bounce to Disk, or you can export individual clips using the Export Clips as Files command.

MP3

It's fast and easy to export from Pro Tools in MP3 format.

To export from Pro Tools in the MP3 format:

1   Do one of the following:

  – Choose FILE > BOUNCE TO > DISK.

  – Select the file(s) you wish to export, and choose EXPORT CLIPS AS FILES from the Clip List menu.

2   In the Bounce (or Export Selected) window, choose MP3 from the File Type pop-up menu, and click BOUNCE (or EXPORT). The MP3 Export options dialog box will appears.

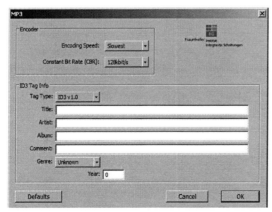

MP3 export options

3   Choose an encoding speed and bit rate, and enter metadata that will be included in the file (see the next section for more information about these options).

4 When finished, click OK.

Export Options

The MP3 export options windows has two Encoder options and a number of fields for inputting information about the file.

- Encoding Speed—There are two options to choose from in this menu: FASTEST and SLOWEST. The Slowest setting should only be used when the highest fidelity is essential, as it can take up to 5 times longer to encode than the Fastest setting.

- Constant Bit Rate (CBR)—This setting determines the data rate (bandwidth) required to play back the file at normal speed. The lower this number, the more data compression must be applied, and therefore the lower the sound quality. At bit rates below 80kbps, the sample rate is also reduced. Commonly used CBR values for stereo music are 128, 160, and 192kbps.

- ID3 Tag Info—The ID3 system allows you to include metadata, or "tags," as part of the MP3 file, which allows MP3 players and software to read information about the program material. The Tag Type pop-up menu lets you choose earlier versions of the ID3 protocol, for compatibility with earlier mp3 players. ID3 2.3 is widely supported and has the distinct advantage that the tag is at the start of the file, allowing a player to display information as soon as the file starts playing.

Windows Media Audio

Export and Bounce to Windows Media format is only available on Windows-based Pro Tools systems.

To export from Pro Tools in the Windows Media format:

1   Do one of the following:

 – Choose FILE > BOUNCE TO > DISK.

 – Select the file(s) you wish to export, and choose EXPORT CLIPS AS FILES from the Clip List menu.

2   In the Bounce (or Export Selected) window, choose WINDOWS MEDIA from the File Type pop-up menu, and click BOUNCE (or EXPORT). The Windows Media export options dialog box will appear.

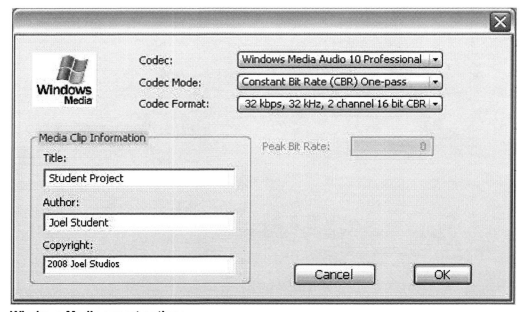

Windows Media export options

Choose a codec, codec mode, and codec format, and add any required information to be embedded in the file, then click OK.

Export Options

The Windows Media export dialog box includes selectors for the Codec (compression/decompression), Codec Mode, and Codec Format options, along with fields for inputting clip information about the file.

- Codec—Windows Media 9 offers 4 basic codecs for compressing audio, as summarized in the following table:

Codec	Notes
Windows Media Audio 9.2	Basic format for most purposes. Data rates up 192kbps at 44.1/48K 16 bit
Windows Media Audio 10 Professional	Higher bit rates up to 440kbps, 24 bits, with 96k support
Windows Media Audio 9 Voice	Low sample rate and data rate (up to 20kbps) for speech-based program material
Windows Media Audio 9.2 Lossless	No audio compression, and up to 96K sample rate. Data compression of 2:1 or 3:1

Note: For extensive information about the Windows Media Audio codecs, visit http://www.microsoft.com/windows/windowsmedia/forpros/codecs/audio.aspx

Depending on the codec chosen, different sets of options will be made available under the Codec Mode and Codec Format pop-up menus.

- Codec Mode—This selector lets you choose between variable and constant bit rate and make speed vs quality decisions. A constant bit rate uses the same amount of data to encode each second of audio, but variable bit rate compression can use different amounts of data depending on the complexity of the program material. VBR compression can produce better results for a given average data rate, but CBR gives you a predictable file size and data rate.

- Codec Format—This is where you choose a sample rate, a data rate (in kilobits per second), and the number of channels. The Professional and Lossless codecs can save multi-channel (surround) audio files.

- Media Clip Information—These fields let you include information about the title, author, and copyright status of the audio. This data is embedded in the file and is displayed by Windows Media Player when the file is played.

Mirrored Outputs

Often you need to send your mix to more than one destination for recording, for example to a DAT and a CD recorder. A studio patchbay may be able to set this routing up outside of Pro Tools, but you can also configure Pro Tools to send your mix to more than one pair of outputs. For example, if your stereo mix path is going to Outputs 1 and 2 of an HD I/O, you can also send it out of Outputs 3 and 4. This is an important skill, as Master Faders are often the last part of your signal path in the Pro Tools mixer, and Master Faders cannot be used to route audio signals.

The process you use to mirror outputs will vary depending on your audio interface(s) and your hardware setup.

Mirroring on TRS Outputs (HD OMNI Only)

In a typical setup, Analog Outputs 1-2 of the HD OMNI will be used for the Main Control Room Monitoring Path, as configured under the Monitor page of the Hardware Setup. This configuration allows you to use the Monitor Encoder on the front panel to adjust the output level for the main mix.

In this scenario, you cannot mirror the main mix (Monitoring Path) on additional primary outputs, as you would with other HD interfaces (see below). However, you can use the TRS Out 1 and 2 jacks on the back panel of the interface to mirror the main mix on Analog Outputs 1-2.

Example: Assigning the TRS Out jacks to mirror Analog Outputs 1-2:

1   Open the Hardware Setup and choose the ANALOG OUT page for the HD OMNI.

2   On the left side of the page under TRS MIRRORS, select ANALOG OUT 1-2.

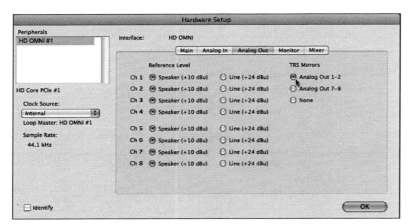

Mirroring outputs 1-2 to the TRS outputs on HD OMNI

3   Click OK to apply the change and close the Hardware Setup dialog box. The main mix from Outputs 1-2 will be mirrored on TRS Out 1 and 2, and both sets will be affected by the Monitor Encoder setting.

Mirroring on Primary Outputs

An alternative setup on HD OMNI does not make use of the internal Monitor paths, allowing you to instead assign your main mix to any of the primary physical outputs on HD OMNI. In this scenario, you can mirror the main mix on a second pair of outputs of your choosing. This process is the same on all other HD interfaces (e.g., HD I/O, 192 I/O, and 96 I/O).

Example: Assigning the main outputs to Analog 1-2 and Analog 3-4:

1   Open the Hardware Setup and choose the MAIN page of the audio interface you are using for your main outputs (usually the first interface).

—   In this example, output channels 1-2 are assigned to Analog outputs 1-2, channels 3-4 to Analog outputs 3-4, etc.

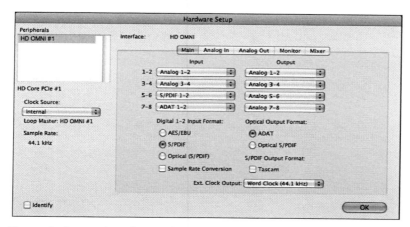

2   If needed, set the channel 3-4 output to NONE in the Output pop-up menu. You need to do this to make Analog outputs 3&4 available to mirror your main outputs.

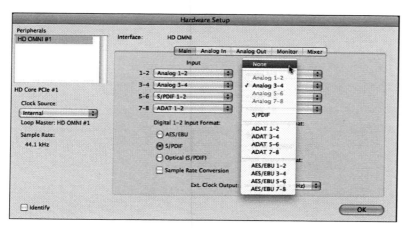

3   Hold CONTROL (Mac) or START (Windows) while choosing the pop-up menu for channels 1-2, and while holding the key, select Analog 3-4 from the pop-up menu. The outputs will be mirrored, and a "+" symbol will display in the assignment pop-up, indicating that more than one assignment is active.

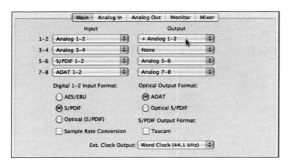

The two outputs will now be identical, and the signal will go to both sets of analog outputs post the master fader for outputs 1-2.

More: In Pro Tools 310M you'll learn how to send different versions of your mix (for example with different vocal balances) to different outputs.

Review Questions

1   What types of systems support exporting MP3 files (Mac/Windows)? What types support WMA exports? (See "MP3/WMA Export" on page 252.)

2   Why might you want to mirror the stereo mix going to Outputs 1 and 2 onto Outputs 3 and 4? (See "Mirrored Outputs" on page 256.)